DEATH IS ONLY A SHORT SEPARATION

I know that my testimony is true; hence, when I talk to these mourners, what have they lost? Their relatives and friends are only separated from their bodies for a short season: their spirits which existed with God have left the tabernacle of clay only for a little moment, as it were; and they now exist in a place where they converse together the same as we do on the earth. (Joseph Smith, JD 6:6.)

HOW WE DIE IS UNIMPORTANT

God, in his eternal decrees, has ordained that all men must die, but as to the mode and manner of our exit, it matters very little. (John Taylor, JD 17:131.)

DEATH REWARDS THE RIGHTEOUS

When I see a man or woman, a true and faithful Latter-day Saint pass away, I do not feel in my heart to mourn. Why should we mourn for the woman whose remains lie before us? She has been true and faithful to the sacred and holy covenants that she entered into with God her Heavenly Father; she has received those ordinances in the house of God that will prepare her to go into the presence of the best men and women that lived upon the earth; she has left a noble posterity to bear her name and to bear record of and to emulate her example; she is freed from pain and suffering and the anxieties of life and is now beyond the power of the enemy of all righteousness; she has opened her eyes in the spirit world, among her relatives and friends and her own little ones, whose death caused her grief and pain; she has gone to enjoy the society of those who have washed their robes and made them white in the blood of the Lamb, and to inherit the blessings and glory of eternal life. No, I cannot feel to mourn for her. It is hard, of course, to part with our friends....It is natural for us to give expression to our feelings in tears in laying away the bodies of our beloved friends. (Wilford Woodruff, JD 22:348.)

DEATH OF INFANTS·

...The Lord takes many away, even in infancy, that they may escape the envy of man, and the sorrows and evils of this present world; they were too pure, too lovely, to live on earth; therefore, if rightly considered, instead of mourning we have reason to rejoice as they are delivered from evil, and we shall soon have them again. (Joseph Smith, DPJS, 113.)

ON THE LOSS OF LITTLE ONES

There are many of our Latter-day Saint mothers who have mourned the loss of their little children, and many mothers have felt that they themselves had committed some great sin, else their little ones would not be taken from them. Now, to such mothers let me say, do not accuse the Lord of taking your little ones from you, nor feel that you have committed any great sin, that those little ones are taken from you, because the Lord loves little children and he will not treat them unkindly, nor without mercy, for through the blood of his atonement they shall come forth in the morning of the resurrection with his saints, and they shall be glorified according to the works they would have accomplished in the earth had they lived. (Hyrum G. Smith, CR April 1917, 70-71.)

DEATH COMES TO ALL

Who is there that can stay the hand of death? What talent, what ingenuity, what philosophy, religion, science or power of any kind? Who possesses that power,... to say to the great monster death, "Stand back, thou shalt not take thy victims"? There is no such person, there is no such power, no such influence, such a principle does not exist, and it never will exist until the last enemy is destroyed, which the scriptures tell us is death. But death shall be destroyed, and all then, even all the human family, shall burst the barriers of the tomb and come forth. (John Taylor, JD 15:348.)

DEBT

ON TIME IS NOT ADVISED

I find a great many people run into debt to buy stock in corporations that I have happened to be president of. When they received good dividends they were glad that they were in the company. But when they were struck financially, I had a great many of them come to me and say, "You are president of this company; I want you to buy my stock." Of course I was not in a position to buy it.

We cannot tell all that is coming in the future. But there is one thing that we can tell, and that is if we have the money in our hands to buy a radio, automobile, or anything else, and we buy it, no matter how much it comes down in value it is ours. (Heber J. Grant, RSM 19:300.)

GET OUT OF DEBT AND KEEP OUT OF DEBT

May I add again an admonition: Live within your means. Get out of debt. Keep out of debt. Lay by for a rainy day which has always come and will come again. Practice and increase your habits of thrift, industry, economy, frugality. Remember that the parable of the ten virgins, the five that were wise and the five that were foolish, can be just as applicable to matters of the temporal world as those of the spiritual. (J. Reuben Clark, Jr., CR October 1937, 107.)

PAY YOUR DEBTS AS SOON AS YOU CAN

If there is anyone here who is in debt I would advise that when he goes home, and when I go home, too, that we will begin with a determination that we will pay our debts and meet all of our obligations just as quickly as the Lord will enable us to do it. If there is anyone here intending to go into debt for speculation, and especially if he is intending to borrow money to buy mining stock and other scaly or uncertain things, I would advise him to hesitate, pray over it, and carefully consider it before he obligates himself by borrowing money and going into debt. In other words, keep out of debt if you can. Pay your debts as soon as you can. That means me as well as anyone else. (Joseph F. Smith, CR October 8, 1911.)

INTEREST IS A HARD TASKMASTER

It is a rule of our financial and economic life in all the world that interest is to be paid on borrowed money. May I say something about interest?

Interest never sleeps nor sickens nor dies; it never goes to the hospital; it works on Sundays and holidays; it never takes a vacation; it never visits nor travels; it takes no pleasure; it is never laid off work nor discharged from employment; it never pays taxes; it buys no food; it wears no clothes; it is unhoused and without home and so has no washing, it has neither wife, children, father, mother, nor kinfolk to watch over and care for; it has no expense of living; it has neither weddings nor births nor deaths; it has no love, no sympathy; it is as hard and soulless as a granite cuff. Once in debt, interest is your companion every minute of the day and night; you cannot shun it or slip away from it; you cannot dismiss it; it yields neither to entreaties, demands, or orders; and whenever you get in its way or cross its course or fail to meet its demands, it crushes you.

So much for the interest we pay. Whoever borrows should understand what interest is; it is with them every minute of the day and night. (J. Reuben Clark, Jr., CR April 1938, 102-103.)

DEBT

"[One] reason for increase in debt... is the rise of materialism, as contrasted with commitment to spiritual values. Many a family, in order to make a 'proper showing,' will commit itself for a larger and more expensive house than is needed, in an expensive neighborhood. Almost everyone would, it seems, like to keep up with the Joneses .... As a result, there is a growing feeling, unfortunately, that material things should be had now, without waiting, without saving, without self denial" (Ezra Taft Benson, ES, June 1987, 3-4.)

LIVE WITHIN YOUR MEANS

I do hope and trust that we Latter-day Saints will live up to the instructions that we have heard so often from this stand, by every president of this Church; that is, to live within our means and keep out of debt. It is a hard thing to do, particularly if we live on the plane that has been set so high, I was going to say, in modern days; but to have peace of mind, happiness within the home, confidence among yourselves, keep out of debt; live within your means; and I know of no people anywhere that can do it so well as the Latter-day Saints, if they will. (Levi Edgar Young, CR April 1934, 57-58.)

DEGREES OF GLORY

JOSEPH SMITH'S VIEWS REGARDING THE VISION OF GLORIES

Nothing could be more pleasing to the Saints upon the order of the kingdom of the Lord, than the light which burst upon the world through the foregoing vision [Doctrine and Covenants, Section 76]. Every law, every commandment, every promise, every truth, and every point touching the destiny of man, from Genesis to Revelation, where the purity of the scriptures remain unsullied by the folly of men, go to show the perfection of the theory [of different degrees of glory in the future life] and witness the fact that the document is a transcript from the records of the eternal world. The sublimity of the ideas; the purity of the language; the scope for action; and continued duration for completion, in order that the heirs of salvation may confess the Lord and bow the knee; the rewards for faithfulness, and the punishments for sins, are so much beyond the narrow-mindedness of men, that every man is constrained to exclaim: "It came from God." (Joseph Smith, DPJS, 136.)

MANY MANSIONS PROVIDED

This earth, this creation, will become a heaven. The heavens that exist now are innumerable to man. God has from all eternity been organizing, redeeming and perfecting creations in the immensity of space; all of which, when they are sanctified by celestial law, and made new and eternal, become the abode of faithful former inhabitants, who also become immortal, through and by celestial law. They are the mansions referred to by the Savior-"In my Father's house are many mansions." In other words, we may say, In our Father's dominions are many mansions. They are not like mansions built by men, they are worlds of greater and lesser magnitude. The first grade are exalted, celestial bodies, from which celestial light will radiate through the immensity of space. (Orson Pratt, JD 18:322.)

ETERNAL GRADES OF PROGRESSION

Those who have not attained to [the celestial kingdom], but can obey a terrestrial law, will receive a terrestrial glory, and enjoy a terrestrial kingdom, and so on. But I believe, furthermore, that there are eternal grades of progression, which will continue worlds without end, and to an infinity of enjoyment, expansion, glory, progression, and of everything calculated to ennoble and exalt mankind. (John Taylor, JD 1:159.)

TELESTIAL, TERRESTRIAL, AND CELESTIAL GLORIES

The glory of the telestial world no man knows, except he partakes of it; and yet, in that world they differ in glory as the stars in the firmament differ one from the other. The terrestrial glory is greater still, and the celestial is the greatest of all; that is the glory of God the Father, where our Lord Jesus Christ reigns. (Brigham Young, JD 6:293.)

COMPARISON OF GLORIES

No man will receive a celestial glory unless he abides a celestial

law; no man will receive a terrestrial glory unless he abides a terrestrial law, and no man will receive a telestial glory unless he
abides a telestial law. There is a great difference between the light
of the sun at noonday and the glimmer of the stars at night, but
that difference is no greater than the difference of the glory in the
several portions of the kingdom of God. (Wilford Woodruff, JD 17:250.)

GLORIES OF SUN, MOON, AND STARS

We read in the Bible that there is one glory of the sun, another
glory of the moon, and another glory of the stars. In the book of
Doctrine and Covenants these glories are called telestial, terrestrial, and celestial, which is the highest. These are worlds, different
departments, or mansions, in our Father's house. (Brigham Young, JD
1:312.)

DEVIL

REBELLION OF THE DEVIL

The contention in heaven was-Jesus said there would be certain
souls that would not be saved; and the devil said he would save
them all, and laid his plans before the grand council, who gave
their vote in favor of Jesus Christ. So the devil rose up in rebellion
against God, and was cast down, with all who put up their heads
for him. (Joseph Smith, DPJS, 130.)

THE FALL OF LUCIFER

One-third part of the spirits that were prepared for this earth
rebelled against Jesus Christ, and were cast down to the earth, and
they have been opposed to him from that day to this, with Lucifer
at their head. He is their general-Lucifer, the son of the morning.
He was once a brilliant and influential character in heaven, and we
will know more about him hereafter. (Brigham Young, JD 5:54-55.)

THE DEVIL CANNOT BE BLAMED FOR OUR SINS

He [Joseph Smith] then observed that Satan was generally
blamed for the evils which we did, but if he was the cause of all
our wickedness, men could not be condemned. The devil could not
compel mankind to do evil; all was voluntary. Those who resisted
the Spirit of God, would be liable to be led into temptation, and
then the association of heaven would be withdrawn from those

who refused to be made partakers of such great glory. God would not exert any compulsory means, and the devil could not; and such ideas as were entertained [on these subjects] by many were absurd. (Joseph Smith, DPJS, 131.)

WE MUST BATTLE SATAN EVERY DAY

The men and women who desire to obtain seats in the celestial kingdom will find that they must battle with the enemy of all righteousness every day. (Brigham Young, JD 11:14.)

A LINE OF DEMARCATION

I have many times repeated what my grandfather said .... In advising his family he said, "there is a line of demarcation, well defined. On one side of the line is the Lord's territory. On the other side of the line is the devil's territory." And he said, "If you will stay on the Lord's side of the line, you are perfectly safe, because the adversary of all righteousness cannot cross the line."

What does that mean? It means to me that those who are living righteous lives, keeping all the commandments of our Heavenly Father, are perfectly safe, but not those who trifle with his advice and counsel. (George Albert Smith, CR September 1949, 5-6.)

POWER OF SATAN TO RISE WITH THE SPREAD OF THE GOSPEL

It was revealed to me in the commencement of this Church, that the Church would spread, prosper, grow and extend, and that in proportion to the spread of the gospel among the nations of the earth, so would the power of Satan rise. It was told you here that Brother Joseph warned the elders of Israel against false spirits.... It was not only revealed to Joseph but to your humble servant, that false spirits would be as prevalent and as common among the inhabitants of the earth as we now see them. (Brigham Young, JD 13:280.)

THE DEVIL AND THE SPIRIT WORLD

Is a saint subject to the power of the devil in the spirit world? No, because he has gained the victory through faith, and can command Satan and he must obey. How is it with the wicked? The devil has power over them to distress and afflict them; they are in hell. (Brigham Young, JD 7:174.)

DIVORCE

DIVORCE UNDER EXTREME CONDITIONS ONLY
Except in cases of infidelity or other extreme conditions, the Church frowns upon divorce, and authorities look with apprehension upon the increasing number of divorces among members of the Church. (David O. McKay, IE 46:657.)

BREAKING THE MARRIAGE TIE-A SAD EXPERIENCE
When we refer to the breaking of the marriage tie, we touch upon one of the saddest experiences of life. For a couple who have basked in the sunshine of each other's love to stand by daily and see the clouds of misunderstanding and discord obscure the love-light of their lives is tragedy indeed. In the darkness that follows, the love sparkle in each other's eyes is obscured. To restore it, fruitless attempts are made to say the right word and to do the right thing; but the word and act are misinterpreted, and angry retort reopens the wound, and hearts once united become torn wider and wider asunder. When this heart-breaking state is reached, a separation is sought. But divorce is not the proper solution, especially if there are children concerned. (David O. McKay, IE 56:657, 704.)

THE SERIOUS EVIL OF DIVORCE
One of the serious evils of our day is divorce, the breaking up of families, the infidelity of husband and wife. There are fewer divorces among the Latter-day Saints than among other people; and in our communities the divorce rate is lower among members of our Church who have been properly married in the temple, as compared with those married by civil ceremony, showing that the teachings of the gospel of Jesus Christ when observed, tend to make the marriage covenant sacred and thereby the evil of divorce is greatly lessened. (Heber J. Grant, IE 44:329.)

DOCTRINE AND COVENANTS

THE WORTH OF THE DOCTRINE AND COVENANTS
In the last [conference] which was held at Brother Johnson's, in

Hiram, after deliberate consideration, in consequence of the book of revelations, now to be printed, being the foundation of the Church in these last days and a benefit to the world, showing that the keys of the mysteries of the kingdom of our Savior are again entrusted to man, and the riches of eternity within the compass of those who are willing to live by every word that proceedeth out of the mouth of God-therefore the conference voted that they prize the revelations [Doctrine and Covenants] to be worth to the Church the riches of the whole earth, speaking temporally. (Joseph Smith, DPJS, 243.)

GLORIOUS PRINCIPLES FOUND IN THE DOCTRINE AND COVENANTS

I say to my brethren that the book of Doctrine and Covenants contains some of the most glorious principles ever revealed to the world, some that have been revealed in greater fullness than they were ever revealed before to the world; and this, in fulfillment of the promise of the ancient prophets that in the latter times the Lord would reveal things to the world that had been kept hidden from the foundation thereof; and the Lord has revealed them through the Prophet Joseph Smith. (Joseph F. Smith, CR October 1913, 9.)

SOLEMN, GODLIKE PRINCIPLES IN DOCTRINE AND COVENANTS

I consider that the Doctrine and Covenants, our testament, contains a code of the most solemn, the most Godlike proclamations ever made to the human family. (Wilford Woodruff, JD 22: 146.)

WONDERFUL REVELATIONS CONTAINED IN THE DOCTRINE AND COVENANTS

I wish that I had the ability to impress upon the Latter-day Saints the necessity of searching the commandments of God, the revelations from the Lord, the Creator of heaven and earth, as contained in the Doctrine and Covenants. If we as a people would live up to those wonderful revelations that have come to us, we would be a bright and shining light to all the wide world. (Heber J. Grant, CR October 1927, 4.)

DOCTRINES

THE DOCTRINES WE HAVE EMBRACED ARE PERFECT

A visitor who was about returning to the Eastern States, said… "You, as a people consider that you are perfect?" "Oh, no;" said I, "Not by any means. Let me define to you. The doctrine that we have embraced is perfect; but when we come to the people, we have just as many imperfections as you can ask for. We are not perfect; but the gospel that we preach is calculated to perfect the people so that they can obtain a glorious resurrection and enter into the presence of the Father and the Son." (Brigham Young, JD 11:304.)

ALL DOCTRINES TO BE REVEALED IN OUR TIME

This is… a day in which the God of heaven has begun to restore the ancient order of his kingdom unto his servants and his people–a day in which all things are concurring to bring about the completion of the fullness of the gospel, a fullness of the dispensation of dispensations, even the fullness of times; a day in which God has begun to make manifest and set in order in his Church those things which have been, and those things which the ancient prophets and wise men desired to see but died without beholding them; a day in which those things begin to be made manifest, which have been hid from before the foundation of the world, and which Jehovah has promised should be made known in his own due time unto his servants, to prepare the earth for the return of his glory, even a celestial glory, and a kingdom of priests and kings to God and the Lamb, forever, on Mount Zion, and with him the hundred and forty and four thousand whom John the Revelator saw, all of which is to come to pass in the restitution of all things. (Joseph Smith, DPJS, 234-235.)

PREACH ONLY THAT WHICH IS KNOWN

With regard to doctrinal points, that which we do not understand should not be talked about in this stand; and the elders of Israel should never contend about any point of doctrine that does not pertain to the present day's salvation. (Brigham Young, JD 7:47.)

DO NOT GO BEYOND WHAT THE LORD HAS REVEALED

If you do not understand a doctrine or a portion of scripture, when information is asked of you, say that the Lord has not revealed that to you, or that he has not opened your understanding to grasp it, and that you do not feel safe in giving an interpretation until he does. (Brigham Young, JD 8:56.)

WHERE TO EXPECT FALSE DOCTRINE

Among .the Latter-day Saints, the preaching of false doctrines disguised as truths of the gospel, may be expected from people of two classes, and practically from these only; they are:

First-The hopelessly ignorant, whose lack of intelligence is due to their indolence and sloth, who make but feeble effort, if indeed any at all, to better themselves by reading and study; those who are afflicted with a dread disease that may develop into an incurable malady-laziness.

Second-The proud and self-vaunting ones, who read by the lamp of their own conceit; who interpret by rules of their own contriving; who have become a law unto themselves, and so pose as the sole judge of their own doings. More dangerously ignorant than the first.

Beware of the lazy and the proud; their infection in each case is contagious; better for them and for all when they are compelled to display the yellow flag of warning, that the clean and uninfected may be protected. (Joseph F. Smith, JI 41:178.)

BEWARE OF TEACHERS OF "NEW PRINCIPLES"

Many imbibe the idea that they are capable of leading out in teaching principles that never have been taught. They are not aware that the moment they give way to this hallucination the devil has power.over them to lead them onto unholy ground; though this is a lesson which they ought to have learned long ago, yet it is one that was learned by but few in the days of Joseph. (Brigham Young, JD 3:318.)

EARTH

THIS EARTH FORMED OUT OF OTHER PLANETS

The world and earth are not synonymous terms. The world is

the human family. This earth was organized or formed out of other planets which were broken up and remodeled and made into one on which we live. The elements are eternal .... In the translation "without form and void," it should read, "empty and desolate." The word created should be "formed or organized." (Joseph Smith, CDG 271 .)

CREATION OF THE EARTH

There is an eternity before us, and it is full of matter; and if we but understand enough of the Lord and his ways, we would say that he took of this matter and organized this earth from it. How long it has been organized it is not for me to say, and I do not care anything about it... whether he made it in six days or in as many millions of years, is and will remain a matter of speculation in the minds of men unless he gives revelation on the subject. If we understood the process of creation there would be no mystery about it, it would all be reasonable and plain, for there is no mystery except to the ignorant. (Brigham Young, JD 14:116.)

FUTURE OF THIS EARTH

This earth, after wading through all the corruptions of men, being cursed for his sake and not permitted to shed forth its full luster and glory, must yet take its proper place in God's creations; be purified from that corruption under which it has groaned for ages and become a fit place for redeemed men, angels, and God to dwell upon. (John Taylor, GG 82.)

THIS EARTH THE PROPERTY OF OUR HEAVENLY FATHER

This earth is the property of our Heavenly Father. Some day it will be cleansed and purified by fire. All disease and sorrow will be banished from it and it will become the celestial kingdom. (George Albert Smith, DNCS June 17, 1944.)

THE EARTH TO BECOME A URIM AND THUMMIM

I remarked to my family and friends present that when the earth was sanctified and became like a sea of glass, it would be one great Urim and Thummim, and the saints could look in it and see as they are seen. (Joseph Smith, HC 5:279.)

EARTH LIFE

EARTH LIFE AND ITS PURPOSE

The greatest lesson you can learn is to know yourselves. When we know ourselves, we know our neighbors. When we know precisely how to deal with ourselves, we know how to deal with our neighbors. You have come here [to earth] to learn this. You cannot learn it immediately, neither can all the philosophy of the age teach it to you; you have to come here to get a practical experience and to know yourselves. You will then begin to learn more perfectly the things of God. No being can thoroughly know himself, without understanding more or less of the things of God; neither can any being learn and understand the things of God, without knowing himself: he must know himself, or he never can know God. (Brigham Young, JD 8:334.)

THE OBJECT IN RECEIVING A BODY

The object of man's taking a body is that through the redemption of Jesus Christ both soul and body may be exalted in the eternal world, when the earth shall be celestial, and obtain a higher exaltation than he could be capable of doing without a body. For when man was first made, he was made "a little lower than the angels." But through the atonement and resurrection of Jesus Christ he is placed in a position to obtain an exaltation higher than angels. For, says the Apostle, "Know ye not that we shall judge angels...."

Another object that we came here for and took bodies was to Propagate our species. For if it is for our benefit to come here, it is also for the benefit of others.

Hence the first commandment given to man was to "Be fruitful and multiply, and replenish the earth." (Gen. 1:28.)(John Taylor, MS 13:81)

OUR GOAL-TO BECOME LIKE CHRIST

The grand object of our coming to this earth is that we may become like Christ, for if we are not like him, we cannot become the sons of God, and be joint heirs with Christ. (Joseph F. Smith, JD 23:172-173.)

WE MUST OVERCOME EVIL TEMPTATIONS

We have been placed here for a purpose. That purpose is that we may overcome the evil temptations that are placed in our way, that we may learn to be charitable to one another, that we may overcome the passions with which we are beset, so that when the time comes for us to go to the other side we may be worthy, by reason of the effort we have put forth, to enjoy the blessings that our Father has in store for the faithful. (George Albert Smith, CR April 1905.)

EDUCATION

THE PURPOSE FOR CHURCH SCHOOLS

The one and only reason why there was any necessity for a Church school was to make Latter-day Saints. It if were only for the purpose of gaining secular knowledge or improving in art, literature, science, and invention, so far as our information was concerned, and adding to it on these subjects,... there was no need of Church schools, because we could gain these things from our secular schools supported by the taxation of the people; and... we had an abundance of uses for all the means that the Church possesses, all the tithing that might come into our hands, without expending vast sums of money upon Church schools. But if we kept in our minds the one central thing, namely, the making of Latter-day Saints in our schools, then they would be fulfilling the object of their existence. The amount of money expended would cut no figure at all, because we cannot value in dollars and cents the saving of a single soul. (Heber J. Grant, IE 24:866-867.)

TRUE EDUCATION COMES FROM GOD

There is no ingenious mind that has ever invented anything beneficial to the human family but what he obtained it from the one Source, whether he knows or believes it or not. There is only one source whence men obtain wisdom, and that is God, the fountain of all wisdom; and though men may claim to make their discoveries by their own wisdom, by meditation and reflection, they are indebted to our Father in heaven for all. (Brigham Young, JD 13:148.)

TRUE EDUCATION AND ZION OF THE LATTER DAYS

You will see the day that Zion will be as far ahead of the outside world in everything pertaining to learning of every kind as we are today in regard to religious matters. You mark my words, and write them down, and see if they do not come to pass. We are not dependent upon them, but we are upon the Lord. We did not get our priesthood nor our information in regard to his law from them. It came from God ....

I remember talking with some celebrated scientists from Europe some time ago, and I explained to them some of the principles relative to the heavenly bodies that were revealed through the Prophet Joseph Smith. They were astonished to know that ideas so grand could be developed through one that was comparatively unlearned. One of them remarked that they were the most magnificent principles he had ever heard of. Another one said that he had read and studied a great deal, but he had a good deal more yet to learn. We are, as the French would say, en rapport with God; that is, in communication with God. Let us live so that we can keep that up, so that angels can minister to us and the Holy Spirit dwell with us. (John Taylor, JD 21:100.)

THE CHURCH STANDS FOR EDUCATION

The Church stands for education. The very purpose of its organization is to promulgate truth among men. Members of the Church are admonished to acquire learning by study, and also by faith and prayer, and to seek after everything that is virtuous, lovely, of good report, or praiseworthy. In this seeking after truth they are not confined to narrow limits of dogma or creed, but are free to launch into the realm of the infinite, for they know that

> Truth is truth where'er 'tis found,
> On Christian or on heathen ground.

Indeed, one of the fundamental teachings of the Church is that salvation itself depends upon knowledge; for, says the revelation, "It is impossible for a man to be saved in ignorance," (D&C 131:6) and again, "... if a person gains more knowledge and intelligence in this life through his diligence and obedience than another, he will have so much the advantage in the world to come." (D&C 130:19.) (David O. McKay, GI 440.)

ETERNAL INCREASE

POWER TO PROPAGATE ONE'S SPECIES

After men have got their exaltations and their crowns-have

become Gods, even the sons of God-are made King of kings and Lord of lords, they have the power then of propagating their species in spirit; and that is the first of their operations with regard to organizing a world. Power is then given to them to organize the elements, and then commence the organization of tabernacles. (Brigham Young, JD 6:275.)

PARENTS OF SPIRITUAL OFFSPRING

So far as the stages of eternal progression and attainment have been made known through divine revelation, we are to understand that only resurrected and glorified beings can become parents of spirit offspring. Only such exalted souls have reached maturity in the appointed course of eternal life; and the spirits born to them in the eternal worlds will pass in due sequence through the several stages or estates by which the glorified parents have attained exaltation. (Joseph F. Smith, IE 19:942.)

FATHERS OF LIVES

The Lord has blessed us with the ability to enjoy an eternal life with the Gods, and this is pronounced the greatest gift of God. The gift of eternal life, without a posterity, to become an angel, is one of the greatest gifts that can be bestowed; yet the Lord has bestowed on us the privilege of becoming fathers of lives. What is a father of lives as mentioned in the scriptures? A man who has a posterity to an eternal continuance. That is the blessing Abraham received, and it perfectly satisfied his soul. He obtained the promise that he should be the father of lives. (Brigham Young, JD 8:63.)

HOW TO HAVE AN ETERNAL INCREASE

Except a man and his wife enter into an everlasting covenant and be married for eternity, while in this probation, by the power and authority of the Holy Priesthood, they will cease to increase when they die; that is, they will not have any children after the resurrection. But those who are married by the power and authority of the priesthood in this life, and continue without appeal to the appetite, our social system would be open to less severe censure than it is today.

In the meantime, let the Church continue its work in the interest of true education; and the Church schools and Sunday Schools ever keep before them the fact that only in true education lies the safety of the home, the state, and the nation, and that "In God's word we have a perfect standard both of duty and character, that by the influence of both, appealing to the best principles of our nature, we may be roused to the noblest and best efforts." (David O. McKay, IE 46:584-585.)

ETERNAL PRINCIPLES

THE PRINCIPLE OF ETERNAL EXISTENCE

I want to reason more on the spirit of man; for I am dwelling on the body and spirit of man-on the subject of the dead. I take my ring from my finger and liken it unto the mind of man-the immortal part, because it had no beginning. Suppose you cut it in two; then it has a beginning and an end; but join it again, and it continues one eternal round. So with the spirit of man. As the Lord liveth, if it had a beginning, it will have an end. (Joseph Smith, DPJS, 124.)

GOD AND MAN ARE ETERNAL BEINGS

All the fools and learned and wise men from the beginning of creation, who say that the spirit of man had a beginning, prove that it must have an end; and if that doctrine is true, then the doctrine of annihilation would be true. But if I am right, I might with boldness proclaim from the house-tops that God never had the power to create the spirit of man at all. God himself could not create himself. (Joseph Smith, DPJS, 125.)

THE DOCTRINE OF ETERNALISM

We are not connected with a something that will exist only for a few years, some of the peculiar ideas and dogmas of men, some nice theory of their forming. The principles that we believe in reach back into eternity. They originated with the Gods in the eternal worlds, and they reach forward to the eternities that are to come. We feel that we are operating with God in connection with those who were, with those who are, and with those who are to come. (John Taylor, JD 17:206.)

WE ARE IN ETERNITY

There is no life more precious than the present life which we enjoy; there is no life that is worth any more to us than this life is.

It may be said that an eternal life is worth more. We are in eternity, and all that we have to do is to take the road that leads into the eternal lives. Eternal life is an inherent quality of the creature, and nothing but sin can put a termination to it. The elements in their nature are as eternal as are the gods. Let us learn, under the guidance and direction of heaven, how to use these eternal elements for the building up, establishment and sending forth, of the kingdom of God, gathering up the poor in heart to begin with, and the further things we will learn as we progress. (Brigham Young, JD 10:22.)

ETERNAL PROGRESSION

THE PRINCIPLE OF ETERNAL PROGRESSION

... The scriptures inform us that Jesus said, as the Father hath power in himself, even so hath the Son power-to do what? Why, what the Father did. The answer is obvious-in a manner to lay down his body and take it up again. Jesus, what are you going to do? To lay down my life as my Father did, and take it up again. Do you believe it? If you do not believe it you do not believe the Bible. The scriptures say it and I defy all the learning and wisdom and all the combined powers of earth and hell together to refute it. Here, then, is eternal life-to know the only wise and true God; and you have got to learn how to be gods yourselves, and to be kings and priests to God, the same as all gods have done before you, namely, by going from one small degree to another, and from a small capacity to a great one; from grace to grace, from exaltation to exaltation, until you attain to the resurrection of the dead, and are able to dwell in everlasting burnings, and to sit in glory, as do those who sit enthroned in everlasting power. And I want you to know that God, in the last days, while certain individuals are proclaiming his name, is not trifling with you or me. (Joseph Smith, DPJS, 40-41.)

THE SELF-EXISTENT PRINCIPLE

The first principles of man are self-existent with God. God himself, finding he was in the midst of spirits and glory, because he was more intelligent, saw proper to institute laws whereby the rest could have a privilege to advance like himself. The relationship we have with God places us in a situation to advance in knowledge. He has power to institute laws to instruct the weaker intelligences, that they may be exalted with himself, so that they might have one glory upon another, and all that knowledge, power, glory, and intelligence, which is requisite in order to save them in the world of spirits. (Joseph Smith, DPJS, 45-46.)

INDIVIDUAL PROGRESSION NECESSARY FOR EXALTATION

Some might suppose that it would be a great blessing to be taken and carried directly into heaven and there set down, but in reality that would be no blessing to such persons; they could not reap a full reward, could not enjoy the glory of the kingdom, and could not comprehend and abide the light thereof, but it would be to them a hell intolerable and I suppose would consume them much quicker than would hell fire. It would be no blessing to you to be carried into the celestial kingdom, and obliged to stay therein, unless you were prepared to dwell there. (Brigham Young, JD 3:221.)

ABILITY TO LEARN WILL INCREASE

I shall not cease learning while I live, nor when I arrive in the spirit world; but shall there learn with greater facility; and when I again receive my body, I shall learn a thousand times more in a thousand times less time; and then I do not mean to cease learning, but shall still continue my researches. (Brigham Young, JD 8:10.)

ETERNAL PROGRESSION A FUNDAMENTAL PRINCIPLE OF THE GOSPEL

If there was a point where man in his progression could not proceed any further, the very idea would throw a gloom over every intelligent and reflecting mind. God himself is still increasing and progressing in knowledge, power, and dominion, and will do so, worlds without end. It is just so with us. (Wilford Woodruff, JD 6:120.)

MUCH TO BE LEARNED BEYOND THE GRAVE

When you climb up a ladder, you must begin at the bottom, and ascend step by step, until you arrive at the top; and so it is with the principles of the gospel-you must begin with the first, and go on until you learn all the principles of exaltation. But it will be a great while after you have passed through the veil before you will have learned them. It is not all to be comprehended in this world; it will be a great work to learn our salvation and exaltation even beyond the grave. (Joseph Smith, DPJS, 138.)

EVIL

THE PLAN OF THE EVIL ONE

These days through which we are now passing, present many problems which are new to all of us but are particularly strange to the younger generation-those who have little background of experience and whose knowledge is limited and immature. Infidelity, atheism, unchastity, intemperance, civil corruption, greed, avarice, ambition-personal, political, national-are more powerful today than at any other time in the lives of us now living. They are pulling and thrusting us almost at will into new fields of action, new lines of thought. They are shaking the faith, undermining the morals, polluting the lives of the people. They have thrown many so far off balance in all of their activities, economic, social, political, and religious, that they stand in real danger of falling. Satan is making war against all the wisdom that has come to men through their ages of experience. He is seeking to overturn and destroy the very foundations upon which society, government and religion rest. He aims to have men adopt theories and practices which he induced their forefathers, over the ages, to adopt and try, only to be discarded by them when found unsound, impractical and ruinous. He plans to destroy liberty and freedom, economic, political and religious, and to set up in place thereof the greatest, most widespread and most complete tyranny that has ever oppressed men. He is working under such perfect disguise that many do not recognize either him or his methods. There is no crime he would not commit, no debauchery he would not set up, no plague he would not send, no heart he would not break, no life he would not take, no soul he would not destroy. He comes as a thief in the night, he is a wolf in sheep's clothing. Without their knowing it, the people are being urged down paths that lead only to destruction. Satan never before had so firm a grip on this generation as he has now. (The First Presidency-Heber J. Grant, J. Reuben Clark, Jr., David O. McKay, IE 45:761.)

EVIL AND ITS TRANSMISSION

Infidels will say to you: "How unjust, how unmerciful, how un-Godlike it is to visit the iniquities of the parents upon the children to the third and fourth generations of them that hate God." How do you see it? This way; and it is strictly in accordance with God's law. The infidel will impart infidelity to his children if he can. The whoremonger will not raise a pure, righteous posterity. He will impart seeds of disease and misery, if not of death and destruction, upon his offspring, which will continue upon his children and descend to his children's children to the third and fourth generation. It is perfectly natural that the children should inherit from their fathers, and if they sow the seeds of corruption, crime and loathsome disease, their children will reap the fruits thereof. Not in accordance with God's wishes, for his wish is that men will not sin and therefore will not transmit the consequences of their sin to their children, but that they will keep his commandments, and be free from sin and from entailing the effects of sin upon their offspring; but inasmuch as men will not hearken unto the Lord, but will become a law unto themselves, and will commit sin they will justly reap the consequences of their own iniquity, and will naturally impart its fruits to their children to the third and fourth generation. The laws of nature are the laws of God, who is just; it is not God that inflicts these penalties, they are the effects of disobedience to his law. The results of men's own acts follow them. (Joseph F. Smith, CR October 1912, 9.)

WHEN TEMPTED GO TO THE LORD

I have seen men tempted so sorely that finally they would say, "I'll be damned if I'll stand it any longer." Well, you will be damned if you do not. So you had better bear it and go to the Lord and say: "O God, I am sorely tempted; Satan is trying to destroy me, and things seem to be combined against me. 0 Lord, help me! Deliver me from the power and grasp of the devil. Let thy Spirit descend upon me that I may be enabled to surmount this temptation and to ride above the vanities of this world." This would be far better than giving way to sin, and proving yourself unworthy of the association of the good and pure. (John Taylor, JD 22:318.)

WE SHOULD RESIST EVIL IN THE WORLD

Sin is in the world, but it is not necessary that we should sin, because sin is in the world; but, to the contrary, it is necessary that we should resist sin, and for this purpose is sin necessary. Sin exists in all the eternities. Sin is co-eternal with righteousness, for it must needs be that there is an opposition in all things. (Brigham Young, JD 10:2.)

EVIL SPIRITS

SAINTS CLOSELY WATCHED BY EVIL SPIRITS
Every person who desires and strives to be a saint is closely watched by fallen spirits that came here when Lucifer fell, and by 'the spirits of wicked persons who have been here in tabernacles and departed from them, but who are still under the control of the prince of the power of the air. Those spirits are never idle; they are watching every person who wishes to do right and are continually prompting them to do wrong. (Brigham Young, JD 7:239.)

LEGIONS OF EVIL SPIRITS
Where will those go to that reject this gospel? Why, in reality they will not go anywhere. They will remain where they are, in hell, where my spirit was for a short time, when I was in England. Where was my body during that brief period? It was in Preston, on the corner of Wilford Street, but my spirit could see and observe those evil spirits as plainly as it ever will after I die. Legions of disembodied evil spirits came against me, organized in companies, that they might have more power, but they had no power over me to any great extent because of the power that was in and sustaining me. I had the priesthood and the power of it was upon me. I saw the invisible world of the condemned spirits, those who were opposed to me and to this work, and to the lifting up of the standard of Christ in that country. Did I at the same time see or have a vision of the angels of God, of his legions? No, I did not; though they were there and stood in defense of me and my brethren, and I knew it. And all this, not that there was any very great virtue in me but there was virtue in the priesthood and apostleship which I held, and God would and did defend; and the evil spirits were dispersed by the power of God.

When I recovered I sat upon the bed, thinking and reflecting upon what had passed, and all at once my vision was opened and the walls of the building were no obstacle to my seeing and I saw nothing but the visions that presented themselves. Why did not the walls obstruct my view? Because my spirit could look through the walls of that house, and I looked with that spirit, element and power with which angels look; and as God sees all things, so were invisible things brought before me as the Lord would bring things before Joseph in the Urim and Thummim. It was upon that principle that the Lord showed things to the Prophet Joseph. (Heber C. Kimball, JD 4:2.)

EXALTATION OF MAN

EXALTATION EXPLAINED

... How consoling to the mourners when they are called to part with a husband, wife, father, mother, child, or dear relative, to know that, although the earthly tabernacle is laid down and dissolved, they shall rise again to dwell in everlasting burnings in immortal glory, not to sorrow, suffer, or die any more, but they shall be heirs of God and joint heirs with Jesus Christ. What is it? To inherit the same power, the same glory and the same exaltation, until you arrive at the station of a god, and ascend the throne of eternal power, the same as those who have gone before. What did Jesus do? Why, I do the things I saw my Father do when worlds came rolling into existence. My Father worked out his kingdom with fear and trembling, and I must do the same; and when I get my kingdom, I shall present it to my Father, so that he may obtain kingdom upon kingdom, and it will exalt him in glory. He will then take a higher exaltation, and I will take his place, and thereby become exalted myself. So that Jesus treads in the tracks of his Father, and inherits what God did before; and God is thus glorified and exalted in the salvation and exaltation of all his children. It is plain beyond disputation, and you thus learn some of the first principles of the gospel, about which so much hath been said. (Joseph Smith, DPJS, 136-137..)

EXALTATION POSSIBLE FOR ALL THE RIGHTEOUS

One of the beautiful things to me in the gospel of Jesus Christ is that it brings us all to a common level. It is not necessary for a man to be a president of a stake, or a member of the Quorum of the Twelve, in order to attain a high place in the celestial kingdom. The humblest member of the Church, if he keeps the commandments of God, will obtain an exaltation just as much as any other man in the celestial kingdom .... In as far as we observe to keep the laws of the Church we have equal opportunities for exaltation. (George Albert Smith, CR October 1933, 25.)

PERFECTION IS TO BECOME LIKE GOD

The man who passes through this probation, and is faithful, being redeemed from sin by the blood of Christ, through the ordinances of the gospel, and attains to exaltation in the kingdom of God, is not less but greater than the angels .... And why? Because the resurrected, righteous man has progressed beyond the pre-existent or disembodied spirits, and' has risen above them, having both spirit and body as Christ has, having gained the victory over death and the grave, and having power over sin and Satan. In fact, having passed from the condition of the angel to that of a god, he possesses keys of power, dominion and glory that the angel does not possess-and cannot possess without gaining them in the same way that he gained .them, which will be by passing through the same ordeals and proving equally faithful .... Man in his pre-existent condition is not perfect, neither is he in the disembodied estate. There is no perfect estate but that of the risen Redeemer, which is God's estate, and no man can become perfect except he become like them [the gods]. (Joseph F. Smith, JD 23:172-173.)

KNOWLEDGE THROUGH JESUS CHRIST IS THE GRAND KEY

Now, there is some grand secret here, and keys to unlock the subject. Notwithstanding the apostle exhorts them to add to their faith, virtue, knowledge, temperance, etc., yet he exhorts them to make their calling and election sure. And though they had heard an audible voice from heaven bearing testimony that Jesus was the Son of God, yet he says we have a more sure word of prophecy, whereunto ye do well that ye take heed as unto a light shining in a dark place. Now, wherein could they have a more sure word of prophecy than to hear the voice of God saying, This is my beloved Son, etc.

Now for the secret and grand key. Though they might hear the voice of God and know that Jesus was the Son of God, this would be no evidence that their election and calling was made sure, that they had part with Christ, and were joint heirs with him. They then would want that more sure word of prophecy, that they were sealed in the heavens and had the promise of eternal life in the kingdom of God. Then, having this promise sealed unto them, it was an anchor to the soul, sure, and steadfast. Though the thunders might roll and lightnings flash, and earthquakes bellow, and war gather thick around, yet this hope and knowledge would support the soul in every hour of trial, trouble, and tribulation. Then knowledge through our Lord and Savior Jesus Christ is the grand key that unlocks the glories and mysteries of the kingdom of heaven. (Joseph Smith, DPJS, 202.)

TO GO WHERE GOD IS WE MUST BE LIKE HIM

If you wish to go where God is, you must be like God, or possess the principles which God possesses, for if we are not drawing towards God in principle, we are going from him and drawing towards the devil. Yes, I am standing in the midst of all kinds of people.

Search your hearts, and see if you are like God. I have searched mine, and feel to repent of all my sins.

We have thieves among us, adulterers, liars, hypocrites. If God should speak from heaven, he would command you not to steal, not to commit adultery, not to covet, nor deceive, but be faithful over a few things. As far as we degenerate from God, we descend to the devil and lose knowledge, and without knowledge we cannot be saved, and while our hearts are filled with evil, and we are studying evil, there is no room in our hearts for good, or studying good. Is not God good? Then you be good; if he is faithful, then you be faithful. Add to your faith virtue, to virtue knowledge, and seek for every good thing. (Joseph Smith, DPJS, 47.)

OBTAIN THE MORE SURE WORD OF PROPHECY

Then I would exhort you to go on and continue to call upon God until you make your calling and election sure for yourselves, by obtaining this more sure word of prophecy, and wait patiently for the promise until you obtain it. (Joseph Smith, DPJS, 150.)

FAITH

BY FAITH ALL THINGS ARE POSSIBLE

Faith is the first principle of revealed religion. It is written that without faith it is impossible to please God. It is also written that the just shall live by faith. Therefore I say it is necessary for all men to have faith in God, the Maker and Creator of all things, the ruler of heaven and earth. Without faith worlds could not have been made; without it they could not be held in their positions; but by faith all things are possible with God and with man. (Joseph F. Smith, MS 57:609.)

FAITH AND ITS FRUITS

... Faith comes by hearing the word of God. If a man has not faith enough to do one thing, he may have faith to do another; if he cannot remove a mountain, he may heal the sick. Where faith is, there will be some of the fruits: all gifts and power which were sent from heaven, were poured out on the heads of those who had faith. (Joseph Smith, DPJS, 86.)

FAITH–A BASIC PRINCIPLE

What is the gospel as taught by Jesus himself?. The very first principle was faith in the Messiah; this was the first principle ever taught to man. When Adam, after being driven from the Garden of Eden, went to Adam-ondi-Ahman to offer sacrifice, the angel of the Lord asked him why he did so. Adam replied that he did not know, but the Lord had commanded him to do it. He was then told that the blood of bulls and goats, of rams and lambs should be spilt upon the altar as a type of the great and last sacrifice which should be offered up for the sins of the world. The first principle, then, ever taught to Father Adam was faith in the Messiah, who was to come in the meridian of time to lay down his life for the redemption of man. (Wilford Woodruff, JD 23:127.)

FAITH IS A GIFT FROM GOD

Faith is a gift of God, and when people have faith to live the gospel, and to listen to the counsel of those who preside in the wards and stakes and of the General Authorities of the Church, it has been my experience that they have been abundantly blessed of the Lord, and that many of them have come out of great financial and other difficulties in a most miraculous and wonderful way. "Obedience is better than sacrifice, and to hearken than the fat of rams." (Heber J. Grant, IE 39:332.)

THE FRUITS OF FAITH

Because faith is wanting, the fruits are. No man since the world has had faith without having something along with it. The ancients quenched the violence of fire, escaped the edge of the sword, women received their dead, etc. By faith the worlds were made. A man who has none of the gifts has no faith; and he deceives himself, if he supposes he has. Faith has been wanting, not only among the heathen, but in professed Christendom also, so that tongues, healings, prophecy, and prophets and apostles, and all the gifts and blessings have been wanting. (Joseph Smith, DPJS, 85-86.)

FAITHFULNESS

FAITHFULNESS REQUIRED BY THE LORD

There are some people who turn back all along the way. ... They cannot make the sacrifice, as they consider it, of paying their tithing. They cannot keep the Word of Wisdom. They cannot be honest, or virtuous or truthful. The result is we find one turning off here, and another there, and leaving the ship of Zion. Now, only those are benefited who continue in their search for salvation, and in their journey toward eternal life. Only those receive a reward who pass through the hardships and the discouraging conditions and continue in the way of life unto the end. If we turn back any time before then, our labors have been in vain and we will not receive the reward. (Abraham O. Woodruff, CR October 1900, 16.)

FAITHFULNESS BRINGS ETERNAL BLESSINGS

The reflection that everyone is to receive according to his own diligence and perseverance while in the vineyard, ought to inspire everyone who is called to be a minister of these glad tidings, to so improve his talent that he may gain other talents, that when the Master sits down to take an account of the conduct of his servants, it may be said, Well done, good and faithful servant: thou hast been faithful over a few things; I will now make thee ruler over many things: enter, thou into the joy of thy Lord. (Joseph Smith, HC 2:6.)

FAITHFULNESS GUIDES ONE INTO THE CELESTIAL KINGDOM

The saints should always remember that God sees not as man sees; that he does not willingly afflict his children, and that if he requires them to endure present privation and trial it is that they may escape greater tribulations which would otherwise inevitably overtake them. If he deprives them of any present blessing it is that he may bestow upon them greater and more glorious ones by and by, and that if counsel does not always result immediately as they had hoped and anticipated, yet, if they will continue to faithfully and unwearingly obey it, it will guide them into the celestial kingdom of the Almighty and lead them back into the presence of their Father and God, where they will enjoy a fullness of all those blessings which their hearts ever desired, and see abundant reason to rejoice that they had received and acted upon the counsel of God's servants. (George Q. Cannon, MS 25:634.)

ENDURE FAITHFULLY TO THE END

Those who endure unto the end shall sit upon thrones as Jesus hath overcome and sat down upon his Father's throne. All things shall be given unto such men and women, so we are told in the revelations we have received. In view of these prospects, what should we not be willing to sacrifice when duty requires? It is a great thing, we say, for a man to be an apostle; yet there are things you can look forward to which are greater than this... The glory that is before us is open to every man and every woman, through this gospel. (Lorenzo Snow, CR October 1898, 55-56.)

FASTING

THE ORIGIN OF THE FAST DAY IN THE CHURCH

How many here know the origin of this day? Before tithing was paid, the poor were supported by donations. They came to Joseph and wanted help, in Kirtland, and he said there should be a fast day, which was decided upon. It was to be held once a month, as it is now, and all that would have been eaten that day, of flour, or meat, or butter, or fruit, or anything else was to be carried to the fast meeting and put into the hands of a person selected for the purpose of taking care of it and distributing it among the poor. If we were to do this now faithfully, do you think the poor would lack for flour, or butter, or cheese, or meat, or sugar, or anything they needed to eat? No, there would be more than could be used by all the poor among us. It is economy in us to take this course, and do better by our poor brethren and sisters than they have hitherto been done by,... The bishops should, through their teachers, see that every family in their wards, who is able, should donate what they would naturally consume on the fast day to the poor. (Brigham Young, 3D 12:115-116.)

THE LAW OF THE. FAST

The law to the Latter-day Saints, as understood by the authorities of the Church, is that food and drink are not to be partaken of for twenty-four hours, "from even to even," and that the Saints are to refrain from all bodily gratification and indulgences. Fast day being on the Sabbath, it follows, of course, that all labor is to be abstained from...

Now, while the law requires the saints in all the world to fast from "even to even," and to abstain both from food and drink it can easily be seen from the scriptures and especially from the words of Jesus, that it is more important to obtain the true spirit of love for God and man, "purity of heart and simplicity of intention," than it is to carry out the cold letter of the law... Many are subject to weakness, others are delicate in health, and others have nursing babies, of such it should not be required to fast. Neither should parents compel their little children to fast... Better teach them the principle, and let them observe it when they are old enough to choose intelligently, than to so compel them. (Joseph F. Smith, IE 6:148-149.)

FASTING, A SPIRITUAL PRINCIPLE

..... Do not think that there is not a spiritual significance in the little principle of fasting. Do not think, parents, that you are favoring your child when, out of compassion, you say, "Oh, give him his breakfast; oh, let us have breakfast; let us have dinner; I have a headache; the little boy is too young to go without his meal," and so on. You do not know what you are doing by such teaching as that. I want to tell you that the children of our Church can be so taught this principle of self-denial that they will set worthy examples to their parents in the observance of it. Your deacons particularly-there is a magnificent opportunity for teaching them one way of honoring the priesthood.

Now, what does obedience to this requirement mean in aiding those who might be in need? It means that money need not be taken from the tithing fund because some of us did not comply with the principle of fast offering! Think what it means, and particularly when we are aiding ourselves by doing it. We are losing nothing financially; we are blessing ourselves physically;and we are gaining greater spiritual power to withstand the temptations that we meet in life; and, best of all, we are practicing the very essence of our religion. (David O. McKay, CR April 1915, 105-106.)

FASTING AND PRAYER

I say to my brethren, when they are fasting and praying for the sick and for those who need faith and prayer, do not go beyond what is wise and prudent in fasting and prayer. The Lord can hear a simple prayer offered in faith, in half a dozen words, and he will recognize fasting that may not continue more than twenty-four hours just as readily and as effectually as he will answer a prayer of a thousand words and fasting for a month. (Joseph F. Smith, CR October 1912, 133-134.)

FOREKNOWLEDGE

FOREKNOWLEDGE OF GOD IS NOT PREDESTINATION

God's foreknowledge concerning the natures and capacities of his children enables him to see the end of their earthly career even from the first: "Known unto God are all his works from the beginning of the world." (Acts 15:18.) Many people have been led to regard this foreknowledge of God as a predestination whereby souls are designated for glory or condemnation even before their birth in the flesh, and irrespective of individual merit or demerit. This heretical doctrine seeks to rob deity of mercy, justice, and love; it would make God appear capricious and selfish, directing and creating all things solely for his own glory, caring not for the suffering of his victims. How dreadful, how inconsistent is such an idea of God! It leads to the absurd conclusion that the mere knowledge of coming events must act as a determining influence in bringing about these occurrences. God's knowledge of spiritual and of human nature enables him to conclude with certainty as to the actions of any of his children under given conditions, yet that knowledge is not of compelling force upon the creature. (James E. Talmage, AF 191.)

FOREKNOWLEDGE DOES NOT CAUSE THINGS TO BE DONE

The gospel reveals many , things to us which others are unacquainted with. I knew of those terrible events which were coming upon this nation previous to the breaking out of our great fratricidal war [Civil War], just as well as I now know that they transpired, and I have spoken of them to many. What of that? Do I not know that a nation like that in which we live, a nation which is blessed with the freest, the most enlightened and magnificent government in the world today, and with privileges which would exalt people to heaven if lived up to-do I not know that if they do not live up to them, but violate them and trample them under their feet and discard the sacred principles of liberty by which we ought to be governed-do I not know that their punishment will be commensurate with the enlightenment which they possess? I do. And I know-I cannot help but know-that there are a great many more afflictions yet awaiting this nation. But would I put forth my hand to help bring them on? God forbid? And you, you Latter-day Saints, would you exercise your influence to the accomplishment of an object of that kind? God forbid! But we cannot help but know these things. But our foreknowledge of these matters does not make us the agents in bringing them to pass. (John Taylor, JD 22:141.)

THE DOCTRINES OF FOREKNOWLEDGE AND FORE-ORDINATION DISCUSSED

Elder J.M. Sjodahl declared that "The doctrine of foreordination, or election as it is also called, appears to me to be set forth in scripture for the purpose of showing us that God acts independently of human advice to bring about his objects and carry out his plans for the benefit of all. It gives us to understand that the success of the kingdom of Christ is absolutely secured, notwithstanding the unbelief and actual enmity of all adversaries. Foreordination takes into consideration repentance, faith, and obedience on the part of man, although unbelief and disobedience cannot prevent, but only retard, the divine plan. God is sovereign in his kingdom; that is the great truth taught as the doctrine of foreordination.

"The true relationship of foreknowledge to foreordination is difficult to explain. God foretells, through his prophets, for instance, the division of the kingdom of Solomon, the captivity of Israel, and the very place of the exile. Human reason would naturally conclude that if God saw that these things were to happen, then they had to happen, no matter what man would do. But history shows that they came about through the sins of the rulers and the people, and that the Lord warned them incessantly against these sins, as if anxious to prevent the predictions from coming true. The very disobedience to the warnings became the immediate justification for the punishment predicted. Could the people have repented and averted the calamities predicted and foreseen? If so, how could they have been foreseen, except conditionally? Perhaps the history of Jonah and Nineveh, by showing that repentance averts disaster even when predicted, offers the only satisfactory answer to that question." (James E. Talmage, AF 490-491.)

FOREORDINATON0N

FOREORDINATION TOOK PLACE IN HEAVEN
Every man who has a calling to minister to the inhabitants of the world was ordained to that very purpose in the Grand Council of heaven before this world was. I suppose that I was ordained to this very office in that Grand Council. It is the testimony that I want that I am God's servant, and this people his people. (Joseph Smith, DPJS, 27.)

FOREORDINATION, A TRUE PRINCIPLE
My faith and feeling about this matter is that we were appointed before the world was, as much as the ancient apostles were, to come forth in the flesh and take hold of this kingdom, and we have it to do, or be damned. (Wilford Woodruff, CR April 1880, 84-85.)

NUMEROUS SAINTS WERE FOREORDAINED
There are thousands of men upon the earth today, among the saints of God, of whom it was decreed before they came that they should occupy the positions they have occupied and do occupy, and many of them have performed their part and gone home; others are left to still fulfill the duties and responsibilities devolving upon them. (John Taylor, JD 23:177.)

JOSEPH SMITH FOREORDAINED TO HEAD THE LAST DISPENSATION
It was decreed in the councils of eternity, long before the foundations of the earth were laid, that he [Joseph Smith] should be the man, in the last dispensation of this world, to bring forth the word of God to the people and receive the fullness of the keys and power of the priesthood of the Son of God. The Lord had his eye upon him and upon his father, and upon his father's father, and upon their progenitors clear back to Abraham, and from Abraham

to the flood, from the flood to Enoch, and from Enoch to Adam. He has watched that family and that blood as it has circulated from its fountain to the birth of that man. He was foreordained in eternity to preside over this last dispensation. (Brigham Young, JD 7:289-290.)

FOREORDINATION NOT PREDESTINATION

It is a mistaken idea... that God has decreed all things whatsoever that come to pass, for the volition of the creature is as free as air. You may inquire whether we believe in foreordination; we do, as strongly as any people in the world. We believe that Jesus was foreordained before the foundations of the world were built, and his mission was appointed him in eternity to be the Savior of the world, yet when he came in the flesh he was left free to choose or refuse to obey his Father. Had he refused to obey his Father, he would have become a son of perdition. We also are free to choose or refuse the principles of eternal life. God has decreed and foreordained many things that have come to pass, and he will continue to do so; but when he decrees great blessings upon a nation or upon an individual they are decreed upon certain conditions. When he decrees great plagues and overwhelming destructions upon nations of people, those decrees come to pass because those nations and people will not forsake their wickedness and turn unto the Lord. It was decreed that Nineveh should be destroyed in forty days, but the decree was stayed on the repentance of the inhabitants of Nineveh...God rules and reigns and has made all his children as free as himself, to choose the right or the wrong, and we shall then be judged according to our works. (Brigham Young, JD 10:324.)

FORGIVENESS

THE PRINCIPLE OF FORGIVENESS

Ever keep in exercise the principle of mercy, and be ready to forgive our brother on the first intimations of repentance, and asking forgiveness; and should we even forgive our brother, or even our enemy, before he repent or ask forgiveness, our Heavenly Father would be equally as merciful unto us. (Joseph Smith, DPJS, 89.)

FORGIVENESS A BASIC DOCTRINE

I believe it is our solemn duty to love one another, to believe in each other, to have faith in each other, that it is our duty to overlook the faults and the failings of each other, and not magnify them in our own eyes nor before the eyes of the world....The - Lord has said-I think I will read it-in one of the revelations, the following:

> Wherefore, I say unto you, that ye ought to forgive one another; for he that forgiveth not his brother his trespasses standeth condemned before the Lord; for there remaineth in him the greater sin.
>
> I, the Lord, will forgive whom I will forgive, but of you it is required to forgive all men.
>
> And ye ought to say in your hearts-let God judge between me and thee, and reward thee according to thy deeds.
>
> And him that repenteth not of his sins, and confesseth them not, ye shall bring before the church, and do with him as the scripture saith unto you, either by commandment or by revelation.
>
> And this ye shall do that God may be glorified-not because ye forgive not, having not compassion, but that ye may be justified in the eyes of the law; that ye may not offend him who is your lawgiver(D&C 64:9-13.)

I believe in that doctrine. We ought not to harbor feelings one against another, but have a feeling of forgiveness and of brotherly .love and sisterly love, one for another. Let each one of us remember his or her own individual failings and weakness and endeavor to correct them. We have not reached a condition of perfection yet; it is hardly to be expected that we will in this life; and yet, through the aid of the Holy Ghost, it is possible for us to stand united together seeing eye to eye and overcoming our sins and imperfections. (Joseph F. Smith, CR April 1915, 119-120.)

BE FORGIVING TO ONE ANOTHER

It is extremely hurtful for any man holding the priesthood, and enjoying the gift of the Holy Ghost, to harbor a spirit of envy, or malice, or retaliation, or intolerance toward or against his fellowmen. We ought to say in our hearts, let God judge between me and thee, but as for me, I will forgive. I want to say to you that Latter-day Saints who harbor a feeling of unforgiveness in their souls are more guilty and more censurable than the one who has sinned against them. Go home and dismiss envy and hatred from your hearts; dismiss the feeling of unforgiveness; and cultivate in your souls that spirit of Christ which cried out upon the cross, "Father, forgive them; for they know not what they do." This is the spirit that Latter-day Saints ought to possess all the day long. The man who has that spirit in his heart and keeps it there will never have any trouble with his neighbor; he will never have any difficulties to bring before the bishop, nor high council; but he will always be at peace with himself, at peace with his neighbors, and at peace with God. It is a good thing to be at peace with God. (Joseph F. Smith, CR October 1902, 86-87.)

WE MUST BE MERCIFUL TO ONE ANOTHER

Suppose that Jesus Christ and holy angels should object to us on frivolous things, what would become of us? We must be merciful to one another, and overlook small things ....

Nothing is so much calculated to lead people to forsake sin as to take them by the hand, and watch over them with tenderness. When persons manifest the least kindness and love to me, O what power it has over my mind, while the opposite course has a tendency to harrow up all the harsh feelings and depress the human mind ....

The nearer we get to our Heavenly Father, the more we are disposed to look with compassion on perishing souls; we feel that we want to take them upon our shoulders, and cast their sins behind our backs .... If you would have God have mercy on you, have mercy on one another. (Joseph Smith, DPJS, 208.)

HAS SOMEBODY OFFENDED YOU IN THE CHURCH?

Has somebody offended you in the Church? You may hold resentment if you wish, say nothing to him, and let resentment canker your soul. If you do, you will be the one who will be injured, not the one who you think has injured you. You will feel better and be far happier to follow the divine injunction: If you have aught against your brother, go to him. (See Matt. 5:23-24.) David O. McKay, DNCS January 2, 1952, 3.)

GATHERING

LAND OF ZION DEDICATED FOR THE GATHERING OF THE SAINTS IN THE LATTER DAYS

On the second day of August [1831], I [Joseph Smith] assisted the Colesville branch of the Church [Colesville branch of the Church numbered about sixty souls] to lay the first log, for a house, as a foundation of Zion in Kaw township, twelve miles west of Independence. The log was carried and placed by twelve men, in honor of the twelve tribes of Israel. At the same time, through prayer, the land of Zion was consecrated and dedicated by Elder Sidney Rigdon for the gathering of the saints. It was a season of joy to those present, and afforded a glimpse of the future, which time will yet unfold to the satisfaction of the faithful. (Joseph Smith, HC 1:196.)

WHY THE SAINTS ARE GATHERED

What was the object of gathering the Jews, or the people of God in any age of the world?...

The main object was to build unto the Lord a house whereby he could reveal unto his people the ordinances of his house and the glories of his kingdom, and teach the people the way of salvation; for there are certain ordinances and principles that, when they are taught and practiced, must be done in a place or house built for that purpose.

It was the design of the councils of heaven before the world was, that the principles and laws of the priesthood should be predicated upon the gathering of the people in every age of the world. Jesus did everything to gather the people, and they would not be gathered, and he therefore poured out curses upon them. Ordinances instituted in the heavens before the foundation of the world, in the priesthood, for the salvation of men, are not to be altered or changed. All must be saved on the same principles.

It is for the same purpose that God gathers together his people in the last days, to build unto the Lord a house to prepare them for the ordinances and endowments, washings and anointings, etc. One of the ordinances of the house of the Lord is baptism for the dead. God decreed before the foundation of the world that that ordinance should be administered in a font prepared for that purpose in the house of the Lord. (Joseph Smith, DPJS, 190.)

GATHERING ESSENTIAL TO THIS DISPENSATION

The gathering of this people is as necessary to be observed by believers as faith, repentance, baptism, or any other ordinance. It is an essential part of the gospel of this dispensation, as much so as the necessity of building an ark by Noah, for his deliverance, was a part of the gospel of his dispensation. (Joseph F. Smith, JD 19:192.)

THE WORK OF GATHERING

All that the prophets that have written, from the days of righteous Abel, down to the last man that has left any testimony on record for our consideration, in speaking of the salvation of Israel in the last days, goes directly to show that it consists in the work of gathering. (Joseph Smith, DPJS, 190-191.)

THE KEYS OF GATHERING

Why is it that you are here today? And what brought you here? Because the keys of the gathering of Israel from the four quarters of the earth have been committed to Joseph Smith, and he has conferred those keys upon others that the gathering of Israel may be accomplished, and in due time the same thing will be performed to the tribes in the land of the north. It is on this account, and through the unlocking of this principle and through these means, that you are brought together as you are today. (John Taylor, JD 25:179.)

GATHERING OF THE SAINTS TO PRECEDE DESTRUCTIONS UPON THE EARTH

Take away the Book of Mormon and the revelations, and where is our religion? We have none; for without Zion, and a place of deliverance, we must fall; because the time is near when the sun will be darkened, and the moon turn to blood, and the stars fall from heaven, and the earth reel to and fro. Then, if this is the case, and if we are not sanctified and gathered to the places God has appointed, with all our former professions and our great love for the Bible, we must fall; we cannot stand; we cannot be saved; for God will gather out his saints from the Gentiles, and then comes desolation and destruction, and none can escape except the pure in heart who are gathered. (Joseph Smith, DPJS, 69.)

THE SAINTS MUST GATHER

The Lord has said by the ancient prophets, in the last days there should be deliverance in Jerusalem and in Mount Zion; and by the mouth of the modern prophet, seer, and revelator, pointed out the location of Zion and commanded the saints among the Gentiles to gather thereunto and build it up, while the Jews gather to Jerusalem. The safety of the saints depends as much upon their fulfilling his commandments as the safety of Noah and Lot depended upon their obedience to the commands of God in their day and generation. (Wilford Woodruff, MS 6:3.)

GATHERING-A PART OF THE RESTORATION OF THE GOSPEL

When the Lord restored the gospel the spirit of gathering came with it. The Lord commanded the people to gather together, and that they should not only be organized as a Church, but that they should be organized under the laws of the land, so that they might 'not be helpless and dependent and without influence or power; but that by means of united effort and faith they should become a power for the accomplishment of righteousness in the earth. (Joseph F. Smith, CR April 1900, 47.)

LAMANITES TO BE GATHERED BY THE GOSPEL

The Book of Mormon has made known who Israel is, upon this continent. And while we behold the government of the United States gathering the Indians, and locating them upon lands to be their own, how sweet it is to think that they may one day be gathered by the gospel! (Joseph Smith, DPJS, 194.)

ALL TRIBES OF ISRAEL TO BE GATHERED

By and by the Jews will be gathered to the land of their fathers, and the ten tribes, who wandered into the north, will be gathered home, and the blood of Ephraim, the second son of Joseph, who was sold into Egypt, will be gathered from among the Gentiles, and the Gentiles who will receive and adhere to the principles of the gospel will be adopted and initiated into the family of Father Abraham, and Jesus will reign over his own and Satan will reign over his own. (Brigham Young, JD 12:38.)

GATHERING OF ISRAEL BEFORE THE LORD COMES

It is... the concurrent testimony of all the prophets, that this gathering together of all the saints, must take place before the Lord comes "to take vengeance upon the ungodly," and "to be glorified and admired by all who obey the gospel." The fiftieth Psalm, from the first to the fifth verse inclusive, describes the glory and majesty of that event. (Joseph Smith, HC 4:272.)

GENTILES

THE NAME GENTILE

The name Gentile is not with us a term of reproach. It comes from Gentilis, meaning of a nation, a family or a people not of Israel-that is all. "Mormon" is a nickname for Latter-day Saints, but "Gentile" is not a nickname. It simply means, with us, one who does not belong to the Church. They are wiser than we are in material things-the things of earth and times. But when it comes to spiritual things—the things of heaven and eternity, we can teach them. We need their wealth and worldly wisdom, their wonderful skill in managing and manipulating temporalities. And they need the gospel and the priesthood. They need us, for we hold in our hands the key to their eternal salvation. (Orson F. Whitney, CR April 1928, 59-60.)

THE EFFECT OF THE HOLY GHOST UPON A GENTILE

The effect of the Holy Ghost upon a Gentile is to purge out the old blood, and make him actually of the seed of Abraham. That man that has none of the blood of Abraham (naturally) must have a new creation by the Holy Ghost. In such a case, there may be more of a powerful effect upon the body, and visible to the eye, than upon an Israelite, while the Israelite at first might be far before the Gentile in pure intelligence. (Joseph Smith, DPJS, 41

TIME OF THE GENTILES

When the British general with his army entered the City of Jerusalem I felt that the time of the Gentiles was very close to being fulfilled. (Heber J. Grant, CR October 1921, 106.)

GENTILES TO RECEIVE GOSPEL FIRST

The great object of the angel in restoring the gospel was, in the first place, to fulfill the times of the Gentiles. Inquires one-"What do you mean by that?" I mean that God will send this gospel, restored by an angel, to every nation, kindred, people and tongue in the Gentile world before he will permit his servants to go to the scattered remnants of Israel. (Orson Pratt, JD 18:176-177.)

GENTILES TO COME IN GREAT NUMBERS

A flowing stream is one that runs continually; and the Gentiles will, in that day, come to us as a flowing stream, and we shall have to set our gates open continually, they will come as clouds and as doves in large flocks. Do you suppose that the Gentiles are going to be ignorant of what is taking place? Now this will not be the case, they will perfectly understand what is taking place. The people will see that the hand of God is over this people; they will see that he is in our midst, and that he is our watchtower, that he is our shield and our defense, and therefore, they will say, "Let us go up and put our riches in Zion, for there is no safety in our own nations."

Those nations are trembling and tottering and will eventually crumble to ruin, and those men of wealth will come here, not to be baptized, but many of them will come that have never heard the servants of God; but they will hear that peace and health dwell among us, and that our officers are all peace officers and our tax-gatherers men of righteousness. (Orson Pratt, JD 3:16.)

GOD

THE KNOWLEDGE OF GOD

God himself was once as we are now, and is an exalted man, and sits enthroned in yonder heavens! That is the great secret. If the veil were rent today, and the great God who holds this world in its orbit, and who upholds all worlds and all things by his power, was to make himself visible-I say, if you were to see him today, you would see him like a man in form-like yourselves in all the person, image, and very form as a man; for Adam was created in the very fashion, image and likeness of God, and received instruction from, and walked, talked, and conversed with him, as one man talks and communes with another. (Joseph Smith, DPJS, 34.)

OUR FATHER IN HEAVEN A GLORIFIED BEING

If we could see our Heavenly Father, we should see a being similar to our earthly parent, with this difference, our Father in heaven is exalted and glorified. He has received his thrones, his principalities and powers, and he sits as a governor, as a monarch, and overrules kingdoms, thrones, and dominions that have been bequeathed to him, and such as we anticipate receiving. While he was in the flesh, as we are, he was as we are. But it is now written of him that our God is as a consuming fire, that he dwells in everlasting burnings, and this is why sin cannot be where he is.

There are principles that will endure through all eternity, and no fire can obliterate them from existence. They are those principles that are pure, and fire is made typical use of to show the glory and purity of the gods, and of all perfect beings. (Brigham Young, JD 4:54.)

WE WILL KNOW OUR HEAVENLY FATHER WHEN WE SEE HIM

If any of us could now see the God we are striving to serve-if we could see our Father who dwells in the heavens, we should learn that we are as well acquainted with him as we are with our earthly father; and he would be as familiar to us in the expression of his countenance and we should be ready to embrace him and fall upon his neck and kiss him, if we had the privilege. And still we, unless the vision of the Spirit is opened to us, know nothing about God. You know much about him, if you did but realize it. And there is no other one item that will so astound you, when your eyes are opened in eternity, as to think that you were so stupid in the body. (Brigham Young, JD 8:30.)

THE FATHER, SON, AND HOLY GHOST SEPARATE PERSONAGES

I have always declared God to be a distinct personage, Jesus Christ a separate and distinct personage from God the Father, and that the Holy Ghost was a distinct personage and a Spirit: and these three constitute three distinct personages and three Gods. (Joseph Smith, DPJS, 35.)

GOD AND THE GODHEAD

There is much said about God and the Godhead. The scriptures say there are gods many and lords many, but to us there is but one living and true God, and the heaven of heavens could not contain him; for he took the liberty to go into other heavens. The teachers of the day say that the Father is God, the Son is God, and the Holy Ghost is God, and they are all in one body and one God. Jesus prayed that those that the Father had given him out of the world might be made one in them, as they were one [one in spirit, in mind, in purpose]. If I were to testify that the Christian world were wrong on this point, my testimony would be true.

Peter and Stephen testify that they saw the Son of Man standing on the right hand of God. Any person that had seen the heavens opened knows that there are three Personages in the heavens who hold the keys of power, and one presides over all. (Joseph Smith, DPJS, 34.)

GOD DWELLS IN EVERLASTING BURNINGS

God Almighty himself dwells in eternal fire; flesh and blood cannot go there, for all corruption is devoured by the fire. "Our God is consuming fire." When our flesh is quickened by the Spirit, there will be no blood in this tabernacle. Some dwell in higher glory than others. (Joseph Smith, DPJS, 223.)

GODS HAVE AN ASCENDANCY OVER ANGELS

Gods have an ascendancy over the angels, who are ministering servants. In the resurrection, some are raised to be angels; others are raised to become gods. These things are revealed in the most holy place in a temple prepared for that purpose. (Joseph Smith, DPJS, 43.)

GODS-MALE AND FEMALE

He made us in the beginning in his own image and in his own likeness, and he made us male and female. We never could be in the image of God if we were not both male and female. Read the scriptures, and you will see it for yourselves as God has made it. He has made us in his own form and likeness, and here we are, male and female, parents and children. (Joseph F. Smith, GD 346.)

THE EXISTENCE OF A PERSONAL GOD

But there are other comprehensive principles to which I wish to call your attention. The first fundamental truth advocated by Jesus Christ was this, that behind, above and over all there is God the Father, Lord of heaven and earth. This universe therefore is not left to the guidance of an irrational, random chance, but on the contrary is ordered and controlled by a marvelous intelligence and wisdom.

Because science says to you young men that it has not found a divine, personal Being, nor the soul of man, are you justified in concluding that these realities do not exist? "There is not a single scientific specialist of repute," says Dr. Hudson, "who has attempted to prove by scientific method that what science cannot demonstrate is thereby disproved." On the contrary, hear ringing these glorious words: "God and the unseen world are not merely objects of surmise. We know them in experience."

Far more direct and impressive are the words of the one in this dispensation who saw God and his Son:

> When the light rested upon me I saw two personages, whose brightness and glory defy all description, standing above me in the air. One of them spake unto me, calling me by name, and said, pointing to the other-This is My Beloved Son. Hear Him!

There is an unchanging truth in an unchanging world, that should be an anchor to the soul of every person in it. (David O. McKay, CR October 1935, 100-101.)

ALLEGIANCE TO GOD

Ours is the great responsibility to become fully involved in the great drive going forward in the Church today: to impress parents with their responsibility to teach their own families in their homes and to have a completely correlated course of gospel teachings in church auxiliaries and priesthood quorums for the children, the youth, and the adults—all to the end that we might develop a gospel scholarship in the individual that will withstand in this evil day the forces that, without this abiding testimony of the gospel, would make us and our children prey to all the vices and false ideologies in the world.

May the Lord continue to pour out his knowledge upon his Church and give to all who are members, and indeed to all the honorable of the earth, attentive minds and obedient hearts, that he may indeed be an ensign to the world as prophesied when "many people shall go and say, Come ye, and let us go up to the mountain of the Lord, to the house of the God o[Jacob; and he will teach us o[his ways, and we will walk in his paths...."(Isa. 2:3.)(Harold B. Lee, CR, April 1966, 68.)

DO NOT "SET UP STAKES FOR THE ALMIGHTY"

I say to all those who are disposed to set up stakes for the Almighty, you will come short of the glory of God. It is the constitutional disposition of mankind to set up stakes and set bounds to the works and ways of the Almighty. (Joseph Smith, DPJS, 201.).

THE THINGS OF GOD ARE OF DEEP IMPORT

The things of God are of deep import; and time, and experience, and careful and ponderous and solemn thoughts can only find them out. Thy mind, 0 man, if thou wilt lead a soul unto salvation, must stretch as high as the utmost heavens, and search into and contemplate the darkest abyss, and the broad expanse of eternity-thou must commune with God. How much more dignified and noble are the thoughts of God, than the vain imaginations of the human heart! (Joseph Smith, DPJS, 72.)

GOOD AND EVIL

ON PORNOGRAPHY

"Teach your children to avoid smut as the plague it is. As citizens, join in the fight against obscenity in your communities. Do not be lulled into inaction by the pornographic profiteers who say that to remove obscenity is to deny people the rights of free choice. Do not let them masquerade licentiousness as liberty.

"Precious souls are at stake—souls that are near
and dear to each of us.

"Sins spawned by pornography unfortunately perpetuate other serious transgressions." (Spencer W. Kimball, ES, Nov. 1976, 6.)

YOU WILL MEET GOLIATHS

"You will meet Goliaths who threaten you. Whether your Goliath is the temptation to steal or destroy or the temptation to rob or the desire to curse and swear; if your Goliath is the desire to wantonly destroy or the temptation to lust and to sin, or the urge to avoid activity, whatever is your Goliath, he can be slain." (Spencer W. Kimball, ES, Nov. 1974, 82)

SIN IS UPON EVERY EARTH

Sin is upon every earth that ever was created, and if it was not so, I would like some philosophers to let us know how people can be exalted to become sons of God and enjoy a fullness of glory with the Redeemer....Every earth and the people thereof, in their turn and time, receive all that we receive and pass through all the ordeals that we are passing through. (Brigham Young, JD 14:71-72.)

BOTH GOOD AND EVIL ARE NECESSARY AND PROPER

It was necessary and proper that there should be good and evil, light and darkness, sin and righteousness, one principle of right opposed to another of wrong, that man might have his free agency to receive the good and reject the evil, and by receiving the good (through the atonement of Jesus Christ and the principles of the gospel), they might be saved and exalted to the eternal Godhead, and go back to their Father and God, while the disobedient would have to meet the consequences of their own acts. (John Taylor, JD 22:301.)

THERE IS NO OTHER WAY TO GIVE MAN EXALTATION

There is not, has not been, and never can be any method, scheme, or plan devised by any being in this world for intelligence to eternally exist and obtain an exaltation, without knowing the good and the evil-without tasting the bitter and the sweet. Can the ,.people understand that it is actually necessary for opposite principles to be placed before them, or this state of being would be no probation, and we should have no opportunity for exercising the agency given us? Can they understand that we cannot obtain eternal life unless we actually know and comprehend by our experience the principle of good and the principle of evil, the light and the darkness, truth, virtue, and holiness-also vice, wickedness, and corruption? (Brigham Young, JD 7:237.)

GOSPEL

THE GOSPEL DOES NOT HAVE TO BE REVISED

There is no need of this people being called together to change the Articles of their Faith, or their creed, for that which they have received is not of man, but from God. It must be very humiliating indeed to a religionist when he thinks upon the fact that his religious sect is forced to call its representatives together from time to time for the purpose of revising its creed, for the reason that the age has outgrown it; that scientific and other discoveries have brought to light certain truths that prove the creeds of fifty or a hundred years ago to be incorrect.

I thank God that this is not the case with Mormonism, and that there has never been,. nor will there ever be, any change in the creed or principles of the system upon which the faith of this people is founded. And this is a grand difference between the work of man and the work of God. That which is of man must be modified and changed to meet the demands of various ages in which mankind live, but that which is of God will endure, as the gospel of Jesus Christ, as revealed through the Prophet Joseph Smith, has endured the scrutiny of critics, the discoveries and the light of science in our day and time. (Abraham O. Woodruff, CR October 1901, 53.)

THE OBJECT OF THE GOSPEL OF JESUS CHRIST

It is conceded by all who have taken the time to study in any degree whatever, the plan of life and salvation and the principles of the gospel of Jesus Christ, on which life and salvation are based, that their object is to develop man so that he will become sufficiently perfected to be worthy to dwell in the presence of our Father in heaven....Every principle of the gospel has been revealed to us for our individual advancement and for our individual perfection. (Heber J. Grant, MS 66:168-169.)

THE GOSPEL OF JESUS CHRIST IS FOR ALL

The Lord has not one gospel for the living and another for the dead, any more than he has one gospel for the Savior and another for his. brethren. The same gospel that saved those before us saves us, and will save those who come after us. (Joseph F. Smith, MS 36:348.)

THE PURPOSE OF THE GOSPEL OF JESUS CHRIST

The purpose of the gospel of Jesus Christ is to prepare us for the celestial kingdom. The Lord has revealed to us that there are other kingdoms of glory and other kingdoms not of glory; but in order that men might be prepared for the celestial kingdom he sent his Only Begotten Son into the world. He, overcame death and found the way of the resurrection, and delivered the message of life and salvation to the children of men....

The only plan that will prepare men for the celestial kingdom is the plan that has been given by Jesus Christ, our Lord. (George Albert Smith, CR April 1934, 28.)

THE GOSPEL OF JESUS CHRIST IS ALL EMBRACING

The gospel embraces principles that dive deeper, spread wider, and extend further than anything else that we can conceive. The gospel teaches us in regard to the being and attributes of God; it also teaches us our relationship to that God and the various responsibilities we are under to him as his offspring; it teaches us the various duties and responsibilities that we are under to our families and friends, to the community, to the living and the dead; it unfolds to us principles pertaining to futurity. In fact, according to the saying of one of the old disciples, it "brings life and immortality to light," brings us into relationship with God, and prepares us for an exaltation in the eternal world. There is something grand, profound and intellectual associated with the principles of the gospel as it stands connected with the salvation and exaltation of man. (John Taylor, JD 16:369-370.)

GREATEST AND MOST IMPORTANT DUTY OF THE CHURCH

After all that has been said, the greatest and most important duty is to preach the gospel. (Joseph Smith, HC 3:478.)

THE GOSPEL HAS THE POWER TO SOLVE WORLD PROBLEMS

The responsibility of showing to the world that the gospel of Jesus Christ will solve its problems rests upon the men who make the claim, who believe that the declaration made by the Prophet Joseph is true. We heard from Brother Stephen L Richards that the Church is so constituted that every human need may be supplied. I believe in his statement. I believe, too, that every world problem may be solved by obedience to the principles of the gospel of Jesus Christ. (David O. McKay, CR April 1920, 116.)

GOVERNMENT

THE POLITICAL MOTTO OF THE CHURCH

The Constitution of our country formed by the Fathers of liberty. Peace and good order in society. Love to God, and good will to man. All good and wholesome laws, virtue and truth above all things, and aristarchy, live forever! But woe to tyrants, mobs, aristocracy, anarchy, and toryism, and all those who invent or seek out unrighteous and vexatious law suits, under the pretext and color of law, or office, either religious or political. Exalt the standard of democracy! Down with that of priestcraft, and let all the people say Amen! that the blood of our fathers may not cry from the ground against us. Sacred is the memory of that blood which bought for us our liberty. (Joseph Smith, DPJS, 304.)

SAINTS TO UPHOLD CONSTITUTIONAL GOVERNMENT

If we would make the world better, let us foster a keener appreciation of the freedom and liberty guaranteed by the government of the United States as flamed by the founders of this nation. Here again self-proclaimed progressives cry out that such old time adherence is out of date. But there are some fundamental principles of this Republic which, like eternal truths, never get out of date, and which are applicable at all times to liberty-loving peoples. Such are the underlying principles of the Constitution, a document framed by patriotic, freedom-loving men, who Latter-day Saints declare were inspired by the Lord ....

There is evidence in the United States of disloyalty to tried and true fundamentals in government. There are unsound economic theories; there are European "isms", which, termite-like, secretly and, recently, quite openly and defiantly, are threatening to undermine our democratic institutions.

Today, as never before, the issue is clearly defined-liberty and freedom of choice, or oppression and subjugation for the individual and for nations. (David O. McKay, CR October 1940, 104-105.)

THE GOVERNMENT OF GOD-A PERFECT SYSTEM

When all nations are so subdued to Jesus that every knee shall bow and every tongue shall confess, there will still be millions on the earth who will not believe in him: but they will be obliged to acknowledge his kingly government. You may call that government ecclesiastical, or by whatever term you please; yet, there is no true government on earth but the government of God, or the Holy Priesthood. Shall I tell you what that is? In short, it is a perfect system of government-a kingdom of gods and angels and all beings who will submit themselves to that government. There is no other true government in heaven or upon the earth. Do not blame me for believing in a pure and holy government. (Brigham Young, JD 7:142.)

GOVERNMENT THROUGH RIGHTEOUSNESS

It has been the design of Jehovah, from the commencement of

the world, and is his purpose now to regulate the affairs of the world in his own time, to stand as a head of the universe and take the reigns of government in his own hand. When that is done judgment will be administered in righteousness; anarchy and confusion will be destroyed, and "nations will learn war no more." It is for want of this great governing principle that all this confusion has existed; "for it is not in man that walketh, to direct his steps;" this we have fully shown. (Joseph Smith, DPJS, 361.)

SAINTS ADVISED TO SUSTAIN THE GOVERNMENT

Sustain the government of the nation wherever you are, and speak well of it, for this is right, and the government has a right to expect it of you so long as that government sustains you in your civil and religious liberty, in those rights which inherently belong to every person born on the earth; and if you are persecuted in your native land, and denied the privilege of worshipping the true God in spirit and in truth, flee to the land of Zion, to America-to the United States, where constitutional rights and freedoms are not surpassed by any nation-where God saw fit, in these last days, to renew the dispensation of salvation, by revelations from the heavens, and where all, by the Constitution and laws of the land, when executed in righteousness, are protected in all the civil and religious freedom that man is capable of enjoying on earth; and our national institutions will never fail, unless it be through the wickedness of the people, and the designs of evil men in brief authority; for those rights were ordained of God on this land, for the establishment of the principles of truth on the earth; and our national organization originated in the heavens. (The First Presidency-Brigham Young, Heber C. Kimball, Willard Richards, MS 14:321ff.)

HOLY GHOST

THE GREATNESS OF THE GIFT OF THE HOLY GHOST

Now, if you have the Holy Ghost with you,... I can say unto you that there is no greater gift, there is no greater blessing, there is no greater testimony given to any man on earth. You may have the administration of angels; you may see many miracles; you may see many wonders in the earth; but I claim that the gift of the Holy Ghost is the greatest gift that can be bestowed upon man. (Wilford Woodruff, DW 38:451.)

HOW THE GIFT OF THE HOLY GHOST IS OBTAINED

There are certain key words and signs belonging to the priesthood which must be observed in order to obtain the blessing. The sign of Peter was to repent and be baptized for the remission of sins, with the promise of the gift of the Holy Ghost; and in no other way is the gift of the Holy Ghost obtained. (Joseph Smith, DPJS, 101.)

KNOWLEDGE OF GOD COMES BY THE HOLY GHOST

President Smith arose and called the attention of the meeting to the 12th chapter 1st Corinthians-"Now concerning spiritual gifts, I would not have you ignorant." Said that the passage in the third verse, which reads, "No man can say that Jesus is the Lord, but by the Holy Ghost," should be translated "No man can know that Jesus is the Lord, but by the Holy Ghost." (Joseph Smith, DPJS, 98.)

THE HOLY GHOST COMES IN THE SIGN OF THE DOVE

Whoever led the Son of God into the waters of baptism, and had the privilege of beholding the Holy Ghost descend in the form of a dove, or rather in the sign of the dove, in witness of that administration? The sign of the dove was instituted before the creation of the world, a witness for the Holy Ghost, and the devil cannot come in the sign of a dove. The Holy Ghost is a Personage, and is in the form of a Personage. It does not confine itself to the form of the dove, but in sign of the dove. The Holy Ghost cannot be transformed into a dove; but the sign of a dove was given to John to signify the truth of the deed, as the dove is an emblem or token of truth and innocence. (Joseph Smith, DPJS, 98.)

THE POWER OF THE HOLY GHOST

Though a man should say but a few words, and his sentences and words be ever so ungrammatical, if he speaks by the power of the Holy Ghost, he will do good. (Brigham Young, JD 8:120.)

DEPENDENCE UPON THE HOLY GHOST

We are all dependent upon the Holy Ghost. And what is the Holy Ghost? The testimony of the Father and the Son. It is one of the Godhead-God the Father, God the Son, and God the Holy Ghost. Will the Holy Ghost deceive any man? It will not. When a man speaks as he is moved upon by the Holy Ghost, it is the spirit of inspiration; it is the word of God; it is the will of God. It cannot lie; it cannot deceive. It leads into all truth, and reveals to man the will of his Maker. (Wilford Woodruff, MS 51:786.)

THE HOLY GHOST IS ONE OF THE GODHEAD

The Lord said, speaking through Joseph Smith: "And whatsoever they shall speak when moved upon by the Holy Ghost, shall be scripture, shall be the will of the Lord, shall be the mind of the Lord, shall be the voice of the Lord, and the power of God unto salvation ."

Why is this? Because the Holy Ghost is one of the Godhead and consequently when a man speaks by the Holy Ghost, it is the word of the Lord. (Wilford Woodruff, MS 51:596.)

DIFFERENCE BETWEEN THE HOLY GHOST AND THE GIFT OF THE HOLY GHOST

There is a difference between the Holy Ghost and the gift of the Holy Ghost. Cornelius received the Holy Ghost before he was baptized, which was the convincing power of God unto him of the truth,of the gospel, but he could not receive the gift of the Holy Ghost until after he was baptized. Had he not taken this sign or ordinance upon him, the Holy Ghost which convinced him of the truth of God, would have left him. (Joseph Smith, DPJS, 100-101.)

THE GIFT OF THE HOLY GHOST A DISTINGUISHING FEATURE OF THE CHURCH

In our interview with the President [Van Buren], he interrogated us wherein we differed in our religion from the other religions of the day. Brother Joseph said we differed in mode of baptism, and the gift of the Holy Ghost by the laying on of hands. We considered that all other considerations were contained in the gift of the Holy Ghost, and we deemed it unnecessary to make many words in preaching the gospel to him. Suffice it to say he has got our testimony. (Joseph Smith, DPJS, 100.)

THE SPIRIT OF THE LORD AND THE HOLY GHOST

The question is often asked, is there any difference between the Spirit of the Lord and the Holy Ghost? ... The Holy Ghost is a Personage in the Godhead and is not that which lighteth every man that comes into the world. It is the Spirit of God which proceeds through Christ to the world, that enlightens every man that comes into the world and that strives with the children of men and will continue to strive with them, until it brings them to a knowledge of the truth and the possession of the greater light and testimony of the Holy Ghost. (Joseph F. Smith, IE 11:381-382.)

POWERFUL DISCOURSES ARE PREACHED BY THE POWER OF THE HOLY PRIESTHOOD AND THE HOLY GHOST

When the Twelve or any other witnesses stand before the congregations of the earth, and they preach in the power and demonstration of the Spirit of God, and the people are astonished and confounded at the doctrine, and say, "That man has preached a powerful discourse, a great sermon," then let that man or those men take care that they do not ascribe the glory unto themselves, but be careful that they are humble, and ascribe the praise and glory to God and the Lamb; for it is by the power of the Holy Priesthood and the Holy Ghost that they have power thus to speak. (Joseph Smith, HC 3:384.)

DO NOT SIN AGAINST THE HOLY GHOST NOR PROVE A TRAITOR TO THE BRETHREN

O ye Twelve and all saints! profit by this important KEY–that in all your trials, troubles, temptations, afflictions, bonds, imprisonments and death, see to it, that you do not betray heaven; that you do not betray Jesus Christ; that you do not betray the brethren; that you do not betray the revelations of God, whether in the Bible, Book of Mormon, or Doctrine and Covenants, or any other that was or ever will be given and revealed unto man in this world or that which is to come. Yea, in all your kicking and flounderings, see to it that you do not this thing, lest innocent blood be found upon your skirts, and you go down to hell. All other sins are not to be compared to sinning against the Holy Ghost, and proving a traitor to the brethren. (Joseph Smith, DPJS, 226.)

HOME

THE STRENGTH OF AMERICAN HOMES

I desire to call attention to the fact that the united, well-ordered American home is one of the greatest contributing factors to the preservation of the Constitution of the United States. It has been aptly said that "Out of the homes of America will come the future citizens of America, and only as those homes are what they should be will this nation be what it should be. (David O. McKay, CR April 1935, 10.)

SET HOMES IN ORDER

Reference has been made to some of the divorces that are increasing in the land. I want to say to you that the larger portion of the divorces are the result of infidelity and immorality, and unfortunately on the part of both men and women. So, brethren, let us set our own homes in order. Let us make our adjustments. Let us live so that we can truthfully look toward the skies and say, "Heavenly Father, we want to be worthy of what you have given to us. We would like to be an example to our neighbors and to all who come in contact with us." And if we will do that, our wives will be true to us, and our children will appreciate us and be true to us. I want to tell you if we want happiness in the celestial kingdom of our God, we will have to lay the foundation for it right here; and part of that requirement of the Lord is that we do right in our homes and live right. Some men think that because they hold the priesthood that that gives them a special way in which they may conduct themselves in their homes. I want to tell you that you men who hold the priesthood will never get into the celestial kingdom, unless you honor your wives and your families and train them and give them the blessings that you want for yourselves.

The fact that they hold the priesthood will be to many men a condemnation, because of the manner in which they have treated it, regarding it as though it were something very ordinary. Priesthood is a word as the titles apostle, prophet, are words and names that ought not to be repeated unnecessarily. We ought to honor these sacred names that bring to us the blessings when we understand. (George Albert Smith, CR April 1948, 183-184.)

WORSHIP IN THE HOME

We have in the gospel the truth. If that is the case, and I bear my testimony that so it is, then it is worth our every effort to understand the truth, each for himself, and to impart it in spirit and practice to our children. Far too many risk their children's spiritual guidance to chance, or to others rather than to themselves, and think that organizations suffice for religious training. Our temporal bodies would soon become emaciated, if we fed them only once a week, or twice, as some of us are in the habit of feeding our spiritual and religious bodies. Our material concerns would be less thriving, if we looked after them only two hours a week, as some people seem to do with their spiritual affairs, especially if we in addition contented ourselves, as some do in religious matters, to let others look after them.

No; on the other hand, this should be done every day, and in the home, by precept, teaching and example. Brethren, there is too little religious devotion, love and fear of God, in the home; too much worldliness, selfishness, indifference and lack of reverence in the family, or these never would exist so abundantly on the outside. Then, the home is what needs reforming. Try today, and tomorrow, to make a change in your home by praying twice a day with your family; call on your children and your wife to pray with you. Ask a blessing upon every meal you eat. Spend ten minutes in reading a chapter from the words of the Lord in the Bible, the Book of Mormon, the Doctrine and Covenants, before you retire, or before you go to your daily toil. Feed your spiritual selves at home, as well as in public places. Let love, and peace, and the Spirit of the Lord, kindness, charity, sacrifice for others, abound in your families. Banish harsh words, envyings, hatreds, evil speaking, obscene language and innuendo, blasphemy, and let the Spirit of God take possession of your hearts. Teach to your children these things, in spirit and power, sustained and strengthened by personal practice. Let them see that you are earnest, and practice what you preach. Do not let your children out to specialists in these things, but teach them by your own precept and example, by your own fireside. Be a specialist yourself in the truth. Let our meetings, schools and organizations, instead of being our only or leading teachers, be supplements to our teachings and training in the home. Not one child in a hundred would go astray, if the home environment, example and training were in harmony with the truth in the gospel of Christ, as revealed and taught to the Latter-day Saints. Fathers and mothers, you are largely to blame for the infidelity and indifference of your children. You can remedy the evil by earnest worship, example, training and discipline, in the home. (Joseph F. Smith, IE 7:135.)

STRENGTHENING THE HOME

We must call ourselves to new service and new responsibilities, and not stand idly by and let these things go without challenge. Our youth are in danger. Keep your home ties strong, brethren. See to it, as we have all tried to say, and as I have repeated it many times and some have quoted it in this conference, that "the greatest of the Lord's work you brethren will ever do as fathers will be within the walls of your own home." Don't neglect your wives, you brethren. Don't neglect your children. Take time for family home evening. Draw your children around about you. Teach them, guide them, and guard them. There was never a time when we needed so much the strength and the solidarity of the home. If we will do that, this church will grow by leaps and bounds in strength and influence throughout the world. (Harold B. Lee, CR April 1973, 130)

IMPORTANCE OF GOOD HOMES

"No nation rises above its homes. In building character the church, the school and even the nation stand helpless when confronted with a weakened and degraded home. The good home is the rock foundation-the cornerstone of civilization. There can be no genuine happiness separate and apart from a good home, with the old-fashioned virtues at its base. If your nation is to endure, the home must be safeguarded, strengthened, and restored to its rightful importance" (Ezra Taft Benson, CR, April 1966, p. 130).

PUT GOD IN YOUR HOME

One day a young son, just married, invited his father to visit him and his bride in their new home. The young son took the father from room to room and showed him the furnishings, the paintings on the walls and so forth, and the father said, "This is lovely. I congratulate you, but, Son, I have looked in vain for anything that indicates that you have a place here for God."

In writing about it later, the young man said, "I went through the rooms later, and I found that Father was right."

Let us go back to our homes and see whether the spirit of our homes is such that if an angel called, he would be pleased to remain. (David O. McKay, CR October 1951, 160-161.)

HONESTY

THE LAW OF HONESTY

"Thou shalt not steal" is one of the commandments.

It is astonishing how many men and women, who have always lived good lives, will yield to temptation to take that which does not belong to them. For the past few years we have been passing through a change. There seems to have been a letting down in the matter of honesty. Our Heavenly Father knew that we would need this commandment when he gave it. It was not given just to be written into the scriptures and then laid upon the shelf. It was given to be proclaimed upon the housetops, if need be....

It is binding upon us today, and I want to say to you that the punishment that is meted out to those who are dishonest, when they are apprehended and hailed before the courts of the land, is insignificant when compared with the spiritual punishment that befalls us when we transgress the law of honesty and violate the commandments of God. (George Albert Smith, JH January 7, 1933.)

HONESTY IS EASIER THAN DECEPTION

Simple truth, simplicity, honesty, uprightness, justice, mercy, love, kindness, do good to all and evil to none, how easy it is to live by such principles! A thousand times easier than to practice deception! (Brigham Young, JD 14:76.)

HONESTY A FUNDAMENTAL PRINCIPLE

The fundamental thing for a Latter-day Saint is to be honest. The fundamental thing for a Latter-day Saint is to value his word as faithfully as his bond; to make up his mind that under no circumstances, no matter how hard it may be, by and with the help of the Lord, he will dedicate his life and his best energies to making good his promise. (Heber J. Grant, IE 41:327.)

HONESTY IN WORSHIP

There is one great principle by which, I think, we all of us ought to be actuated in our worship, above everything else that we are associated with in life, and that is honesty of purpose....

It is proper that men' should be honest with themselves, that they should be honest with each other in all their words, dealings, intercourse, intercommunication, business arrangements, and everything else. They ought to be governed by truthfulness, honesty, and integrity, and that man is very foolish indeed who would not be true to himself, true to his convictions and feelings in regard to religious matters. We may deceive one another, as in some circumstances, counterfeit coin passes for that which is considered true and valuable among men. But God searches the hearts and tries the reins of the children of men. He knows our thoughts and comprehends our desires and feelings. He knows our acts and the motives which prompt us to perform them. He is acquainted with all the doings and operations of the human family, and all the secret thoughts and acts of the children of men are open and naked before him, and for them he will bring them to judgment.

These ideas are believed in by men generally, who, with very few exceptions, whatever their general conduct or ideas on religious matters may be, believe in an all-seeing eye which penetrates and is enabled to weigh the actions and motives of the children of men. This is an idea that will not be disputed by any race of men now existing upon the earth, nor perhaps by any who have existed heretofore, for whatever may have been the theories or notions of men in former times, they have generally had a reverence for, and a belief in, an all-wise, supreme, omnipotent Being, who, they supposed, was greater than all of them, and who governed and controlled all their actions. A feeling of this kind is frequently made manifest in the scriptures, and it is nothing new in our age to believe in a God of this character. (John Taylor, JD 16:301-302.)

HUMILITY

DO NOT PUT YOUR TRUST IN THE ARM OF FLESH

Next to the committing of sin there is no more fruitful cause of apostasy among the Latter-day Saints than when we put our trust in the arm of flesh. I firmly believe that no man who honestly bows down every day of his life and supplicates God in sincerity for the light of his Holy Spirit to guide him will ever become proud and haughty. On the contrary, his heart will become filled with meekness, humility, and childlike simplicity. (Heber J. Grant, JH July 7, 1882.)

THOSE WHO HUMBLE THEMSELVES WILL RECEIVE MORE

Those who humble themselves before the Lord, and wait upon him with a perfect heart and willing mind, will receive little by little, line upon line, precept upon precept, here a little, and there a little, "now and again," as Brother John Taylor says, until they receive a certain amount. Then they have to nourish and cherish what they receive, and make it their constant companion, encouraging every good thought, doctrine and principle and doing every good work they can perform, until by and by the Lord is in them a well of water, springing up unto everlasting life. (Brigham Young, JD 4:286-287.)

IN THE THINGS OF GOD, MAN HAS NO POWER IN HIM-SELF

You may hear many say, "I am a Latter-day Saint, and I never will apostatize;" "I am a Latter-day Saint, and shall be to the day of my death." I never make such declarations, and never shall. I think I have learned that of myself I have no power, but my system is organized to increase in wisdom, knowledge, and power, getting a little here and a little there. But when I am left to myself, I have no power, and my wisdom is foolishness; then I cling close to the Lord, and I have power in his name. I think I have learned the gospel so as to know, that in and of myself I am nothing. In the organization of my system, however, is a foundation laid, if I rightly improve upon it, that will secure to me the independence of the Gods in eternity. This is obtained by strictly adhering to the principles of the gospel in this life, which will lead us on from faith to faith, and from grace to grace. This is the way, I think, I have learned the Lord. (Brigham Young, JD 1:337-338.)

WE MUST GO BEFORE GOD WITH A BROKEN HEART AND CONTRITE SPIRIT

Wherein have we come short of obeying the principles of the gospel? Have I done any injury to my fellowman? Have I grieved the Spirit of the Lord? Have I neglected some duty? Have I said that which I ought not to have said? Have I done that which I ought not to have done? Have I been just, have I been merciful, have I been upright? Have I allowed any thought, any feeling to enter my heart concerning my neighbor, concerning some of my associates that I should not entertain? If I have, then it is my duty, if I believe the gospel and desire to practice its principles, to repent of that, to confess it.

There was a time when God required of his people the sacrifice of animals. They brought their animals and they were offered up as sacrifices, and they obtained the remission of sins by that method. This was required under the law of Moses; it was required until the coming of the Son of God, until he made his great sacrifice for man. But what does God require of us? Is it that we shall bring animals and offer burnt offerings unto him? No, he does not make that requirement of us to-day, but this is the sacrifice required of us: he asks us that we shall come to him with broken hearts and with contrite spirits. If we do he will accept of us, our offerings will be like the offerings of Abel, acceptable in his sight; but if we go to him as Cain did, our offerings will not be acceptable to him, and he will reject them. But if you and I and all who profess to be the followers of the Lord Jesus will bow down before him with humble hearts, each of us with a broken heart and contrite spirit, what will be the effect? Why, we will confess our faults to him, because they will be plain in our sight, we will see ourselves in the light of the Spirit of God, and the spirit of repentance will rest down upon us. (George Q. Cannon, JD 20:289.)

ACT FOR THE GOOD OF EACH OTHER

Again, let the Twelve and all saints be willing to confess all their sins, and not keep back a part; and let the Twelve be humble, and not be exalted, and beware of pride, and not seek to excel one above another, but act for each other's good, and pray for one another, and honor our brother or make honorable mention of his name, and not backbite and devour our brother. (Joseph Smith, HC 3:383-384.)

BE HUMBLE-DO NOT SEEK POSITIONS

He [Joseph Smith] spoke of the disposition of many men to consider the lower offices in the Church dishonorable, and to look with jealous eyes upon the standing of others who are called to preside over them; that it was the folly and nonsense of the human heart for a person to be aspiring to other stations than those to which they are appointed of God for them to occupy; that it was better for individuals to magnify their respective callings, and wait patiently till God shall say to them, "Come up higher." (Joseph Smith, DPJS, 295-296

HUSBANDS

DUTY OF HUSBAND TO WIFE

If there is any man who ought to merit the curse of Almighty God it is the man who neglects the mother of his child, the wife of his bosom, the one who has made sacrifice of her very life, over and over again for him and his children. That is, of course, assuming that the wife is a pure and faithful mother and wife. (Joseph F. Smith, IE 21:105.)

HUSBANDS SHOULD LOVE WIVES

As teachers, we are to let the people know, and warn these men-and this is not imagination-who, after having lived with their wives and brought into this world four and five and six children, get tired of them and seek a divorce, that they are on the road to hell. It is unfair to a woman to leave her that way, merely because the man happens to fall in love with some younger woman and feels that the wife is not so beautiful or attractive as she used to be. Warn him! Nothing but unhappiness for him and injustice to those children can result. (David O. McKay, CR April 1949, 182-183.)

THE RESPONSIBILITY OF HUSBANDS

God expects you to be true to your vows, to be true to yourselves, and to be true to your wives and children. If you become covenant-breakers, you will be dealt with according to the laws of God. And the men presiding over you have no other alternative than to bring the covenant-breaker to judgment. If they fail to do their duty, we shall be under the necessity of looking after them, for righteousness and purity must be maintained in our midst. (John Taylor, JD 24:171-172.)

HUSBANDS SHOULD SET GOOD EXAMPLES

I would like to emphasize tonight something that has been referred to before and that is that men, who have been married to women and have agreed before witnesses that they will keep the commandments of God and live as they should, sometimes are so selfish, so willful, that they forget that their wives have some rights. I want to say that the priesthood does not give any man a right to abuse his wife. The priesthood does give him a right to be kind, to be faithful, to be honorable, to teach the truth and to teach his children the truth, and when he does that he will not fall away into sin. There never has been a time in the history of the world when we have needed divine guidance more than now. (George Albert Smith, CR April 1949, 189.)

HUSBAND AND WIFE RELATIONSHIPS

Husbands, do you love your wives and treat them right, or do you think that you yourselves are some great moguls who have a right to crowd upon them? They are given to you as a part of yourself, and you ought to treat them with all kindness, with mercy and long suffering, and not be harsh and bitter, or in any way desirous to display your authority. Then, you wives, treat your husbands right, and try to make them happy and comfortable. Endeavor to make your home a little heaven, and try to cherish the good Spirit of God. Then let us as parents train up our children in the fear of God and teach them the laws of life. If you do, we will have peace in our bosoms, peace in our families, and peace in our surroundings. (John Taylor, JD 21:118-119.)

KINDNESS OF HUSBANDS TO WIVES

I mention this now, because I think we are sometimes cruel to our wives. I have here two letters, one anonymous, another signed. by a woman. They are asking "What shall we do? Our husbands are cruel to us."

Says one, "My husband has a terrible temper. He comes home and scolds the children. He is cruel to me. At first he seemed to be a good loving husband, but when my first baby was born, then were born my troubles."

I cannot imagine a man's being cruel to a woman. I cannot imagine her so conducting herself as to merit such treatment. Perhaps there are women in the world who exasperate their husbands, but no man is justified in resorting to physical force or in exploding his feelings in profanity. There are men, undoubtedly, in the world who are thus beastly, but no man who holds the priesthood of God shall so debase himself. (David O. McKay, CR October 1951, 181.)

IDLERS

IDLERS HAVE NO PLACE IN ZION

There should be no idlers in Zion. Even the poor who have to be assisted should be willing to do all in their power to earn their own living. Not one man or woman should be content to sit down and be fed, clothed, or housed without any exertion on his or her part to compensate for these privileges. All men and women should feel a degree of independence of character that would stimulate them to do something for a living, and not be idle; for it is written that the idler shall not eat the bread of the laborer of Zion, and he shall not have place among us. Therefore, it is necessary that we should be industrious, that we should intelligently apply our labor to something that is productive and conducive to the welfare of the human family. (Joseph F. Smith, CR April 1899, 42.)

WE WANT TO BANISH IDLENESS

How necessary it is that we should listen to the words of wisdom and instruction which have been given, counseling us to so organize ourselves and arrange our temporal affairs, that there may not be a single individual throughout our land, who desires to work, go unemployed, but that all may have this blessed privilege, for when men labor they keep out of mischief. You remember the old proverb-"An idle man's brain is the devil's workshop." We want to banish. idleness, how shall we do it? By organizing, and every president of stake and every bishop making it the study and object of his life to furnish employment to every man under his immediate presidency who may desire it (George Q. Cannon, JD 20:7.)

CEASE TO BE IDLE

I desire to say to this congregation at this time that I have felt very strongly of late a desire, a responsibility, I may say, resting upon me, to admonish the Latter-day Saints everywhere to cease loitering away their precious time, to cease from all idleness. It is said in the revelations that the idler in Zion shall not eat the bread of the laborer, and there is vastly too much, in some parts-not universally, but there is far too much precious time wasted by the youth of Zion, and perhaps by some that are older and more experienced and who ought to know better, in the foolish, vain and unprofitable practice of cardplaying. We hear of card parties here and card parties there, and entertainments where the playing of cards is the principal amusement; and the whole evening is thus wasted. The whole precious time of those who are gathered together on occasions of this kind, aggregating many hours, absolutely wasted. If there was nothing else to be said against this practice, that alone should be sufficient to induce Latter-day Saints not to indulge in this foolish and unprofitable pastime.

Read good books. Learn to sing and to recite, and to converse upon subjects that will be of interest to your associates, and at your social gatherings, instead of wasting the time in senseless practices that lead only to mischief and sometimes to serious evil and wrongdoing; instead of doing this, seek out of the best books knowledge and understanding. Read history. Read philosophy, if you wish. Read anything that is good, that will elevate the mind and will add to your stock of knowledge, that those who associate with you may feel an interest in your pursuit of knowledge and of wisdom. (Joseph F. Smith, CR October, 98.)

IDLENESS PROMOTES EVIL

My policy is to keep every man, woman, and child busily employed, that they may have no idle time for hatching mischief in the night, and for making plans to accomplish their own ruin.

We see men in our streets employed only in plotting the ruin of this people. But men who are engaged in canyons, in stores, or in any active labor in the daytime, when night comes they are glad to rest. Night is the time the idle and the indolent watch for their prey. My policy is to keep everybody busy in building up this kingdom; in building houses, in breaking up land; in setting out fruit and ornamental trees; in laying out fine gardens, pleasant walks, and beautiful groves; and in building academies, and other places of learning.

There are hundreds of young men here who can go to school, which is far better than to waste their time. Study languages, get knowledge and understanding; and while doing this, get wisdom from God, and forget it not, and learn how to apply it, that you may do good with it all the days of your lives. (Brigham Young, JD 2: 144-145.)

INTELLIGENCE

INTELLIGENCE EXISTS ETERNALLY

The mind or the intelligence which man possesses is co-equal [co-eternal] with God himself ....

I am dwelling on the immortality of the spirit of man. Is it logical to say that the intelligence of spirits is immortal and yet that it had a beginning? The intelligence of spirits had no beginning, neither will it have an end. That is good logic. That which has a beginning may have an end. There never was a time when there were not spirits; for they are co-equal [co-eternal] with our Father in heaven ....

Intelligence is eternal and exists upon a self-existent principle. It is a spirit from age to age, and there is no creation about it. (Joseph Smith, DPJS, 124.)

INTELLIGENCE ACQUIRED HERE IS REGAINED IN LIFE TO COME

I rejoice to know that whatever degree of intelligence we attain unto in this life shall rise with us in the life to come, and we shall have just that much the advantage of those who have not gained intelligence, because of their failure to study diligently. (Heber J. Grant, CR October 1907, 24.)

WHEN A MAN IS FULL OF THE LIGHT OF ETERNITY

I long for the time that a point of the finger, or motion of the hand, will express every idea without utterance. When a man is full of the light of eternity, then the eye is not the only medium through which he sees, his ear is not the only medium by which he hears, nor the brain the only means by which he understands. When the whole body is full of the Holy Ghost, he can see behind him with as much ease, without turning his head, as he can see before him. If you have not that experience, you ought to have. It is not the optic nerve alone that gives the knowledge of surrounding objects to the mind, but it is that which God has placed in man-a system of intelligence that attracts knowledge, as light cleaves to light, intelligence to intelligence, and truth to truth. It is this which lays in man a proper foundation for all education. I shall yet see the time that I can converse with this people, and not speak to them but the expression of my countenance will tell the congregation what I wish to convey, without opening my mouth. (Brigham Young, JD 6:317.)

JESUS CHRIST

CHRIST IN THE IMAGE OF HIS FATHER

We should understand this, that Jesus Christ came into the world, in the meridian of time, to be the Only Begotten Son of God in the flesh. That is a doctrine established in this Church, and we have received it by revelation so we can put aside any doubts or speculations or contentions in regard to it. That was when he came and tabernacled, being in the image of his Father, the "express" image of his Father before he came into the world, and with power, as the heir of all things, God honored him and loved him, and he knew the faithfulness in the work entrusted to him, and knew beforehand what he would do when he came on the earth to be the Redeemer of mankind....Jesus as we call him, the Nazarene, the son of Mary, of the offspring of David, therefore the Son of man, was the Son of God, who is the Father of his spirit. So, in the beginning he was with God and was the firstborn of this great family and on the earth he was the Only Begotten of the Father in the flesh. (Charles W. Penrose, CR April 1921, 10-11.)

JEHOVAH, THE FIRSTBORN

Among the spirit children of Elohim, the firstborn was and is Jehovah, or Jesus Christ, to whom all others are juniors. (Joseph F. Smith, IE 19:940.)

JESUS IS OUR MEDIATOR

Jesus Christ is the medium through whom we are to approach the Father, calling upon him in the name of Jesus; for there is no name given under heaven, nor known among men, whereby we can be saved but the name of Jesus Christ. (John Taylor, JD 20:175.)

JESUS CHRIST THE HEAD OF THE CHURCH

One of our brethren who spoke today gave out the idea that he knew who was to lead the Church. I also know who will lead this Church, and I tell you that it will be no man who will lead The Church of Jesus Christ of Latter-day Saints; I don't care in what time nor in what generation. No man will lead God's people nor his work. God may choose men and make them instruments in his hands for accomplishing his purposes, but the glory and honor and power will be due to the Father, in whom rest the wisdom and the might to lead his people and take care of his Zion. I am not leading the Church of Jesus Christ, nor the Latter-day Saints, and I want this distinctly understood. No man does. Joseph did not do it; Brigham did not do it; neither did John Taylor. Neither did Wilford Woodruff, nor Lorenzo Snow; and Joseph F. Smith, least of them all, is not leading The Church of Jesus Christ of Latter-day Saints, and will not lead it. They were instruments in God's hands in accomplishing what they did. God did it through them. (Joseph F. Smith, CR October 1904, 5.)

CHRIST'S MISSION FULFILLED

The Savior came and tabernacled in the flesh, and entered upon the duties of the priesthood at thirty years of age. After laboring three and a half years he was crucified and put to death in fulfillment of certain predictions concerning him. He laid down his life as' a sacrifice for sin, to redeem the world. When men are called upon to repent of their sins, the call has reference to their own individual sins, not to Adam's transgressions. What is called the original sin was atoned for through the death of Christ irrespective of any action on the part of man; also man's individual Sin was atoned for by the same sacrifice, but on condition of his obedience to the gospel plan of salvation when proclaimed in his hearing. (Wilford Woodruff, MS 51:658-659.)

MISSION OF JESUS CHRIST REGARDING THE CHILDREN OF GOD

The errand of Jesus to earth was to bring his brethren and sisters back into the presence of the Father; he has done his part of the work, and it remains for us to do ours. There is not one thing that the Lord could do for the salvation of the human family that he has neglected to do; and it remains for the children of men to receive the truth or reject it; all that can be accomplished for their salvation, independent of them, has been accomplished in and by the Savior...."Jesus paid the debt; he atoned for the original sin; he came and suffered and died on the cross." (Brigham Young, JD 13:59.)

THE LIFE OF JESUS CHRIST THE SUPREME EXAMPLE OF GOODNESS

I have always looked upon the life of our Savior-who descended beneath all things that he might rise above all things-as an example for his followers. And yet it has always, in one sense of the word, seemed strange to me that the Son of God, the First Begotten in the eternal worlds of the Father, and the Only Begotten in the flesh, should have to descend to the earth and pass through what he did-born in a stable, cradled in a manger, persecuted, afflicted, scorned, a hiss and byword to almost all the world, and especially to the inhabitants of Jerusalem and Judea. There was apparently nothing that the Savior could do that was acceptable in the eyes of the world; anything and almost everything he did was imputed to an unholy influence. When he cast out devils the people said he did it through the power of Beelzebub, the prince of devils; when he opened the eyes of the blind, the Pharisees and priests of the day told the man to "give God the glory; we know this man is a sinner." And so all his life through, to the day of his death upon the cross! There is something about all this that appears sorrowful; but it seemed necessary for the Savior to descend below all things that he might ascend above all things. So it has been with other men. (Wilford Woodruff, JD 23:327.)

NONE PERFECT BUT JESUS

Where is the man that is free from vanity? None ever were perfect but Jesus; and why was he perfect? Because he was the Son of God, and had the fullness of the Spirit, and greater power than any man. (Joseph Smith, DPJS, 43.)

ALL SHALL KNOW JESUS CHRIST

The time will come when every knee will bow and every tongue confess to and acknowledge him, and when they who have lived upon the earth and have spurned the idea of a Supreme Being and of revelations from him, will fall with shamefacedness and humble themselves before him, exclaiming "There is a God! O God, we once rejected thee and disbelieved thy word and set at naught thy counsels, but now we bow down in shame and we do acknowledge that there is a God, and that Jesus is the Christ." This time will come most assuredly. (Brigham Young, JD 13:306-307.)

JESUS CHRIST-THE GREAT HIGH PRIEST

The most precious thing in the world is a testimony of the truth. I repeat, truth never grows old, and the truth is that God is the source of your priesthood and mine; that he lives, that Jesus Christ, the great high priest, stands at the head of this Church, and that every man who holds the priesthood, if he lives properly, soberly, industriously, humbly, and prayerfully, is entitled to the inspiration and guidance of the Holy Spirit. I know that is true. (David O. McKay, CR April 1948, 172.)

FAITH IN GOD

Once we accept Christ as divine, it is easy to visualize his Father as being just as personal as he. Christ said, "He that hath seen me hath seen the Father." (John 14:9.) Faith in the existence of a divine and real and living personal God was the first element that contributed to the perpetuity of the Church of Jesus Christ in ancient times, and it is the everlasting foundation upon which The Church of Jesus Christ of Latter-day Saints is built today. (Howard W. Hunter, ES May 1991, 63.)

CHRIST, THE ANOINTED ONE

The call to come unto him has continued throughout time and is being renewed in our day. Modern scriptures are replete with the same invitation. It is an urgent, pleading call to everyone. Indeed, the calm but urgent appeal is still from the Son of God himself. He is, in fact, the Anointed One who will lift the greatest of burdens from the most heavily laden. The conditions for obtaining that assistance are still precisely the same. We must come unto him and take his yoke upon us. In meekness and lowliness, we must learn of him in order to receive eternal life and exaltation. (Howard W. Hunter, ES, Nov 1990, 18.)

GREATEST SUFFERING WAS IN GETHSEMANE

We speak of the passion of Jesus Christ. A great many people have an idea that when he was on the cross, and nails were driven into his hands and feet, that was his great suffering. His great suffering was before he ever was placed upon the cross. It was in the Garden of Gethsemane that the blood oozed from the pores of his body: "Which suffering caused myself, even God, the greatest of all, to tremble because of pain, and to bleed at every pore, and to suffer both body and spirit—and would that I might not drink the bitter cup, and shrink."

That was not when he was on the cross; that was in the garden. That is where he bled from every pore in his body.

Now I cannot comprehend that pain. I have suffered pain, you have suffered pain, and sometimes it has been quite severe; but I cannot comprehend pain, which is mental anguish more than physical. that would cause the blood, like sweat, to come out upon the body. It was something terrible, something terrific; so we can understand why he would cry unto his Father:

"If it be possible, let this cup pass from me: nevertheless not as I will, but as thou wilt." (Joseph Fielding Smith, D.S., I, 130.)

MY FRIEND, MY SAVIOR

"To the testimonies of these mighty men and Apostles of old- our brethren in the ministry of the same Master– add my own testimony. I know that Jesus Christ is the Son the living God and that he was crucified for the sins of the world.

"He is my friend, my Savior, my Lord, my God." (Spencer W. Kimball, ES, Nov. 1978, p. 73.)

DEATH OF THE SAVIOR AS RECORDED BY JOSEPH SMITH

(April 6, 1833)… The day was spent in a very agreeable / manner, in giving and receiving knowledge which appertained to this last kingdom-it being just 1800 years since the Savior had laid down his life that men might have everlasting life, and only three years since the Church had come out of the wilderness, preparatory for the last dispensation. (Joseph Smith, DPJS, 268)

JEWS AND JERUSALEM

THE JEWS AND THE SECOND COMING OF CHRIST

Judah must return, Jerusalem must be rebuilt, and the temple, and water come out from under the temple, and the waters of the Dead Sea be healed. It will take some time to rebuild the walls of the city and the temple, etc. ;and all this must be done before the Son of Man will make his appearance. (Joseph Smith, DPJS, 236-237.)

GATHERING OF THE JEWS

When the Gentiles reject the gospel it will be taken from them and go to the house of Israel, to that long suffering people that are now scattered abroad through all the nations upon the earth, and they will be gathered home by thousands, and by hundreds of thousands, and they will rebuild Jerusalem their ancient city and make it more glorious than at the beginning, and they will have a leader in Israel with them, a man that is full of the power of God and the gift of the Holy Ghost. (Wilford Woodruff, JD 2:200.)

WEALTHY JEWS TO ASSIST IN GATHERING THEIR PEOPLE

The time is not far distant when the rich men among the Jews may be called upon to use their abundant wealth to gather the dispersed of Judah and purchase the ancient dwelling places of their fathers in and about Jerusalem and rebuild the holy city and temple. For the fullness of the Gentiles has come in, and the Lord has decreed that the Jews should be gathered from all the Gentile nations where they have been driven, into their own land, in fulfillment of the words of Moses their law-giver. (Wilford Woodruff, MS 41:244.)

JEWS TO BE GATHERED FROM GENTILE NATIONS

The Lord has decreed that the Jews should be gathered from all the Gentile nations where they have been driven, into their own land, in fulfillment of the words of Moses their law-giver .... 0 house of Judah,... it is true that after you return and gather your nation home and rebuild your city and temple, that the Gentiles may gather together their armies to go against you to battle, to take you a prey and to take you as a spoil, which they will do, for the words of your prophets must be fulfilled; but when this affliction comes, the living God that led Moses through the wilderness will deliver you, and your Shiloh will come and stand in your midst and will fight your battles; and you will know him, and the afflictions of the Jews will be at an end, while the destruction of the Gentiles will be so great that it will take the whole house of Israel who are gathered about Jerusalem seven months to bury the dead of their enemies, and the weapons of war will last them seven years for fuel, so that they need not go to any forest for wood. These are tremendous sayings-who can bear them? Nevertheless they are true and will be fulfilled, according to the sayings of Ezekiel, Zechariah, and other prophets. Though the heavens and the earth pass away, not one jot or tittle will fall unfulfilled. (Wilford Woodruff, WW 509-510.)

JERUSALEM AND THE LAST DAYS

Zechariah, in his 14th chapter, has told us much concerning the great battle and overthrow of the nations who fight against Jerusalem, and he has said, in plain words, that the Lord shall come at the very time of the overthrow of that army, yes, in fact, 'even while they are in the act of taking Jerusalem, and have already succeeded in taking one-half the city, and spoiling their houses, and ravishing their women. Then, behold their long expected Messiah, suddenly appearing, shall stand upon the Mount of Olives, a little east of Jerusalem, to fight against those nations 'and deliver the Jews. Zechariah says the Mount of Olives shall cleave in twain, from east to west, and one-half of the mountain shall remove to the north, while the other half falls off to the south, suddenly forming a very great valley, into which the Jews shall flee for protection from their enemies as they fled from the earthquake in the days of Uzziah, king of Judah, while the Lord cometh and all the saints with him. Then will the Jews behold that long, long-expected Messiah, coming in power to their deliverance, as they always looked for him. He will destroy their enemies, and deliver them from trouble at the very time they are in the utmost consternation, and about to be swallowed up by their enemies. But what will be their astonishment when they are about to fall at the feet of their Deliverer, and acknowledge him their Messiah! They discover the wounds which were once made in his hands, feet, and sides, and, on inquiry, at once recognize Jesus of Nazareth the King of the Jews, the man so long rejected. Well did the Prophet say, they shall mourn and weep, every family apart, and their wives apart. But, thank heaven, there will be an end to their mourning, for he will forgive their iniquities and cleanse them from uncleanness. Jerusalem shall be a holy city from that time forth, and all the land shall be turned as a plain from Geba to Rimmon, and she shall be lifted up and inhabited in her place, and men shall dwell there, and there shall be no more utter destruction of Jerusalem, "And in that day there shall be one Lord, and his name one, and he shall be King over all the earth." (Zech. 14:9.)

John, in his 11th chapter of Revelation, gives us many more particulars concerning this same event. He informs us that, after the city and temple are rebuilt by the Jews, the Gentiles will tread it under foot forty and two months, during which time there will be two prophets continually prophesying and working mighty miracles. And it seems that the Gentile army shall be hindered from utterly destroying and overthrowing the city, while these two prophets continue. But, after a struggle of three years and a half, they at length succeed in destroying these two prophets, and then overrunning much of the city, they send gifts to each other because of the death of the two prophets, and in the meantime will not allow their dead bodies to be put in graves, but suffer them to lie in the streets of Jerusalem three days and a half, during which the armies of the Gentiles, consisting of many kindreds, tongues and nations, passing through the city, plundering the Jews, see their dead bodies lying in the street. But after three days and a half, on a sudden, the spirit of life from God enters them, and they will arise and stand upon their feet, and great fear will fall upon them that see them. And then they shall hear a voice from heaven saying, "Come up hither," and they will ascend up to heaven in a cloud, and their enemies beholding them. And having described all these things, then comes the shaking, spoken of by Ezekiel, and the rending of the Mount of Olives, spoken of by Zechariah. John says, "The same hour was there a great earthquake, and the tenth part of the city fell, and in the earthquake were slain of men seven thousand." And then one of the next scenes that follows is the sound of voices saying, "The kingdoms of this world are become the kingdom of our Lord, and of his Christ; and he shall reign forever and ever."

Now, having summed up the description of these great events spoken of by these prophets, I would remark, there is no difficulty in understanding them all to be perfectly plain and literal in their fulfillment.

Suffice it to say, the Jews gather home, and rebuild Jerusalem. The nations gather against them in battle. Their armies encompass the city, and have more or less power over it for three years and a half. A couple of Jewish prophets, by their mighty miracles, keep them from utterly overcoming the Jews, until at length they are slain, and the city is left in a great measure to the mercy of their enemies for three days and a half, the two prophets rise from the dead and ascend up into heaven. The Messiah comes, convulses the earth, overthrows the army of the Gentiles, delivers the Jews, cleanses Jerusalem, cuts off all wickedness from the earth, raises the saints from the dead, brings them with him, and commences his reign of a thousand years, during which time his Spirit will be poured out upon all flesh, men and beasts, birds and serpents, will be perfectly harmless and peace and the knowledge and glory of God shall cover the earth as the waters cover the sea; and the kingdom and the greatness of the kingdom under the whole heaven shall be given to the saints of the Most High. (Parley P. Pratt. VW 40-42.)

JUSTICE AND JUDGMENT

MEN WILL BE JUDGED BY THEIR ACTIONS

The sectarian doctrine of final rewards and punishments is as strange to me as their bodiless, partless, and passionless God. Every man will receive according to the deeds done in the body, whether they be good or bad. All men, excepting those who sin against the Holy Ghost, who shed innocent blood or who consent thereto, will be saved in some kingdom; for in my Father's house, says Jesus, are many mansions. (Brigham Young, JD 11:125-126.)

GOD SEARCHES THE HEART

We may deceive one another in some circumstances, as counterfeit coin passes for that which is considered true and valuable among men. But God searches the hearts and tries the reins of the children of men. He knows our thoughts and comprehends our desires and feelings; he knows our acts and the motives which prompt us to perform them. He is acquainted with all the doings and operations of the human family, and all the secret thoughts and acts of the children of men are open and naked before him, and for them he will bring them to judgment. (John Taylor, JD 16:301-302.)

JUDGE NOT

It is not our province as members of the Church, to sit in judgment upon one another and call bad names when we reflect upon the acts of people. We have no right, even if we are in official capacity, to form a one-sided judgment. There are two sides to every such question, if not more, always; and we should hear both, "hear defense before deciding, and a ray of light may gleam,

showing thee what filth is hiding underneath the shallow stream."
Hear the other side before you begin to find fault, and pass judgment....So when we are called upon to sit in judgment, either in a
bishop's court or in a high council (to which the bishop's court
may be appealed), if we are members of the high council, just
remember what the Lord has said concerning such quorum or
council. Every decision of these quorums that are organized must
be given in justice, in righteousness, in equity, in fear of the Lord,
and with the desire to do what is right, not out of personal feeling.
Personal feelings ought to be banished from our souls when we sit
in judgment having the right to sit in judgment. (Charles W. Penrose, CR
October 1916, 21-22.)

JUDGE NOT, THAT YE BE NOT JUDGED

Judge no man. A person who would say another is not a Latter-
day Saint, for some trifling affair in human life proves that he does
not possess the Spirit of God. Think of this, brethren and sisters;
Write it down, that you may refresh your memories with it; carry it
with you and look at it often. If I judge my brethren and sisters,
unless I judge them by the revelations of Jesus Christ, I have not
the Spirit of Christ; if I had, I should judge no man. (Brigham Young,
JD 1:339.)

JESUS CHRIST AND APOSTLES SHALL JUDGE

We may here state that Christ is called the judge of the quick
and the dead, the judge of all the earth. We further read that the
Twelve Apostles who ministered in Jerusalem "shall sit upon
twelve thrones, judging the twelve tribes of Israel." (Matt. 19:28.)

And Nephi writes in the Book of Mormon:

> And the angel spake unto me, saying, Behold the twelve disciples
> of the Lamb, who are chosen to minister unto thy seed; And he said
> unto me, Thou rememberest the twelve apostles of the Lamb? Behold,
> they are they who shall judge the twelve tribes of Israel; wherefore, the
> twelve ministers of thy seed shall be judged of them; for ye are of the
> house of Israel. And these twelve ministers, whom thou beholdest, shall
> judge thy seed. And, behold, they are righteous forever; for because of
> their faith in the Lamb of God their garments are made white in his
> blood. (1 Ne. 12:8-10 .)

This exhibits a principle of adjudication or judgment in the
hands, firstly, of the Great High Priest and King, Jesus of Nazareth,

the Son of God; secondly, in the hands of the Twelve Apostles on the continent of Asia, bestowed by Jesus himself; thirdly, in the Twelve Disciples on this continent, to their people, who it appears are under the presidency of the Twelve Apostles who ministered at Jerusalem; which presidency is also exhibited by Peter, James and John, the acknowledged presidency of the Twelve Apostles; they, holding this priesthood first on the earth, and then in the heavens. Being the legitimate custodians of the keys of the priesthood, they came and bestowed it upon Joseph Smith and Oliver Cowdery. It is also further stated that the saints shall judge the world. Thus Christ is at the head, his apostles and disciples seem to take the next prominent part; then comes the action of the saints, or other branches of the priesthood, who it is stated shall judge the world. This combined Priesthood, it would appear, will hold the destiny of the human family in their affairs; and it would seem to be quite reasonable, if the Twelve Apostles in Jerusalem are to be the judges of the Twelve Tribes, and the Twelve Disciples on this continent are to be the judges of the descendants of Nephi, then that the brother of Jared and Jared should be the judges of the Jaredites, their descendants; and, further, that the First Presidency and Twelve who have officiated in our age, should operate in regard to mankind in this dispensation, and also in regard to all matters connected with them, whether they relate to the past, present, or future, as the aforementioned have done in regard to their several peoples; and that the patriarchs, the presidents, the Twelve, the high priests, the seventies, the elders, the bishops, priests, teachers and deacons should hold their several places behind the veil, and officiate according to their calling and standing in that priesthood. In fact, the priesthood is called an everlasting priesthood- it ministers in time and in eternity. (John Taylor, MA 152-153.)

KINGDOM OF GOD

JOSEPH SMITH AND THE KINGDOM OF GOD

I calculate to be one of the instruments of setting up the kingdom of Daniel by the word of the Lord, and I intend to lay a foundation that will revolutionize the whole world....It will not be by sword or gun that this kingdom will roll on: the power of truth is such that all nations will be under the necessity of obeying the gospel (Joseph Smith, DPJS, 171.)

THE KINGDOM OF GOD DEFINED

What I mean by the kingdom of God is the organization of The Church of Jesus Christ of Latter-day Saints, over which the Son of God presides, and not man. That is what I mean. I mean the kingdom of which Christ is the King and not man. If any man object to Christ, the Son of God, being King of Israel, let him object, and go to hell just as quick as he please. (Joseph F. Smith, CR October 1906, 9.)

WHEN THE KINGDOM OF GOD IS FULLY SET UP

When the kingdom of God is fully set up and established on the face of the earth, and takes the preeminence over all other nations and kingdoms, it will protect the people in the enjoyment of all their rights, no matter what they believe, what they profess, or what they worship. If they wish to worship a God of their own workmanship, instead of the true and living God, all right, if they will mind their own business and let other people alone. (Brigham Young, JD 2:310.)

THE EFFECT OF THE KINGDOM OF GOD

What is the kingdom of God going to accomplish on the earth? It will revolutionize not only the United States, but the whole world, and will go forth from the morning to the evening, from the rising of the sun to the going down of the same, so shall be the ushering forth of the gospel until the whole earth is deluged with it, and the righteous are gathered. (Brigham Young, JD 2:190.)

THE FUTURE OF THE KINGDOM OF GOD

Now as to the great future, what shall we say? Why, a little stone has been cut out of the mountains without hands, and this little stone is becoming a great nation, and it will eventually fill the whole earth. How will it fill it? Religiously? Yes, and politically too, for it will have the rule, the power, the authority, the dominion in its own hands. (John Taylor, JD 9:343.)

SEEING AND ENTERING THE KINGDOM OF GOD

It is one thing to see the kingdom of God, and another thing to enter into it. We must have a change of heart to see the kingdom of God, and subscribe to the articles of adoption to enter therein. (Joseph Smith, DPJS, 171.)

OLD GLORY AND THE KINGDOM OF GOD

When the day comes in which the kingdom of God will bear rule, the flag of the United States will proudly flutter unsullied on the flag staff of liberty and equal rights, without a spot to sully its fair surface; the glorious flag our fathers have bequeathed to us will then be unfurled to the breeze by those who have power to hoist it aloft and defend its sanctity. (Brigham Young, JD 2:317.)

"THY KINGDOM COME"

"Thy kingdom come."... This was taught by Jesus to his disciples when they came to him, saying, teach us to pray....Thy kingdom come. What kingdom? What is the meaning of "thy kingdom come?" It means the rule of God. It means the law of God. It means the government of God. It means the people who have listened to and who are willing to listen to and observe the commandments of Jehovah. And it means that there is a God who is willing to guide and direct and sustain his people. Thy kingdom come, that thy government may be established, and the principles of eternal truth as they exist in the heavens may be imparted to men; and that, when they are imparted to men, those men may be in subjection to those laws and to that government, and live in the fear of God, keeping his commandments and being under his direction. Thy kingdom come, that the confusion, the evil, and wickedness, the murder and bloodshed that now exist among mankind may be done away, and the principles of truth and right, the principles of kindness, charity, and love as they dwell in the bosom of the Gods, may dwell with us. (John Taylor, JD 23:177-178.)

EVERY KNEE SHALL BOW

If the Latter-day Saints think, when the kingdom of God is established on the earth, that all the inhabitants of the earth will join the Church called Latter-day Saints, they are mistaken. I presume there will be as many sects and parties then as now. Still, when the kingdom of God triumphs, every knee shall bow and every tongue confess that Jesus is the Christ, to the glory of the Father. Even the Jews will do it then; but will the Jews and Gentiles be obliged to belong to The Church of Jesus Christ of Latter-day Saints? No; not by any means. Jesus said to his disciples, "In my Father's house are many mansions; were it not so I would have told you; I go to prepare a place for you, that where I am, there ye may be also," etc. There are mansions in sufficient numbers to suit the different classes of mankind, and a variety will always exist to all eternity, requiring a classification and an arrangement into societies and communities in the many mansions which are in the Lord's house, and this will be so for ever and ever. Then do not imagine that if the kingdom of God is established over the whole earth, all the people will become Latter-day Saints. They will cease their persecutions against the Church of Jesus Christ, and they will be willing to acknowledge that the Lord is God, and that Jesus is the Savior of the world. (Brigham Young, JD 11:275.)

WHOSE RIGHT IS IT TO RULE?

It startles men when they hear the elders of Israel tell about the kingdoms of this world becoming the kingdom of our God and his Christ. They say it is treason for men to teach that the kingdom Daniel saw is going to be set up and bear rule over the whole earth. Is it treason for God Almighty to govern the earth? Who made it? God, did he not? Who made you? God, if you have any Eternal Father. Well, whose right is it to rule and reign over you and the earth? It does not belong to the devil, nor to men. It has never been given to men yet; it has never been given to the nations. It belongs solely to God and he is coming to rule and reign over it. (Wilford Woodruff, JD 13:164.)

KNOWLEDGE

KNOWLEDGE OF FACTS NOT ENOUGH

The mere stuffing of the mind with a knowledge of facts is not education. The mind must not only possess a knowledge of the truth, but the soul must revere it, cherish it, love it as a priceless gem; and this human life must be guided and shaped by it in order to fulfill its destiny. The mind should not only be charged with intelligence, but the soul should be filled with admiration and desire for pure intelligence which comes of a knowledge of the truth. The truth can only make him free who hath it and will continue in it. And the word of God is truth, and it will endure forever. (Joseph F. Smith, C 16:570.)

SAINTS ADVISED TO ACQUIRE AND USE KNOWLEDGE

I would urge upon the young men to do nothing for show, but to do their best to obtain knowledge and then strive to put the knowledge obtained to practical use. I am acquainted with some people who are regular encyclopedias of knowledge, but so far as their knowledge being utilized for the benefiting of their fellow men, they might just as well not possess it or be deaf, dumb, and blind; this is all wrong. (Heber J. Grant, IE 3:304.)

HOW TO OBTAIN KNOWLEDGE

It is not wisdom that we should have all knowledge at once presented before us; but that we should have a little at a time; then we can comprehend it....

Add to your faith knowledge, etc. The principle of knowledge is the principle of salvation. This principle can be comprehended by the faithful and diligent; and every one that does not obtain knowledge sufficient to be saved will be condemned. The principle of salvation is given us through the knowledge of Jesus Christ. (Joseph Smith, HC 5:387.)

KNOWLEDGE AND INTELLIGENCE

There is a difference between knowledge and pure intelligence. Satan possesses knowledge, far more than we have, but he has not intelligence or he would render obedience to the principles of truth and right. I know men who have knowledge, who understand the principles of the gospel, perhaps as well as you do, who are brilliant, but who lack the essential qualification of pure intelligence. They will not accept and render obedience thereto. Pure intelligence comprises not only knowledge, but also the power to properly apply that knowledge. (Joseph F. Smith, GD 58.)

TRUE KNOWLEDGE IS FROM GOD

It is good for men to be taught in the history and laws of nations, to become acquainted with the principles of justice and equity, with the nature of disease and the medicinal properties of plants, etc. But there is no need of their being without the knowledge of God, for in fact every branch of true knowledge known to man has originated in God, and men have come in possession of it from his word or from his works. O, the folly of men in not acknowledging God in all things, in laying aside God and his religion, and trusting in their own judgment and intelligence. All the intelligence which men possess on the earth, whether religious, scientific, or political-proceeds from God. Every good and perfect gift proceeds from him, the fountain of light and truth, wherein there is no variableness nor shadow of turning. The knowledge of the human system has proceeded from the human system itself, which God has organized.

Again, if you trace the old English laws and the laws of ancient nations, it will be seen that the principles of justice, which are the foundation of them, are gathered from the Bible, the revealed will of God to the children of Israel for their government and guidance, to a certain extent, in some of the principles of law, justice, and equity. Did knowledge of any kind that is in the world originate in man? No. Franklin possessed great information relating to natural laws. He drew the lightning from the clouds but he could not have done that if there had not been lightning in the clouds. He merely discovered a certain principle, and developed the action of a certain law that existed co-equal with the earth. Then how foolish it is for men under these circumstances, to lay aside God, and think that they can progress, and be smart and intelligent without him. (John Taylor, JD 10:275.)

HOW TO IMPROVE OUR KNOWLEDGE

A man who wishes to receive light and knowledge, to increase in the faith of the holy gospel, and to grow in the knowledge of the truth as it is in Jesus Christ, will find that when he imparts knowledge to others he will also grow and increase. Be not miserly m your feelings, but get knowledge and understanding by freely imparting it to others. (Brigham Young, JD 2:267.)

HOW MEN LOSE KNOWLEDGE

As far as we degenerate from God, we descend to the devil and lose knowledge, and without knowledge we cannot be saved, and while our hearts are filled with evil, and we are studying evil, there is no room in our hearts for good, or studying good....

A man is saved no faster than he gets knowledge, for if he does not get knowledge, he will be brought into captivity by some evil power in the other world, as evil spirits will have more knowledge and consequently more power than many men who are on the earth. Hence it needs revelation to assist us and give us knowledge of the things of God. (Joseph Smith, HC 4:588.)

LAST DAYS

THE SPIRIT OF GOD WILL WITHDRAW FROM GENTILE NATIONS

By and by the Spirit of God will entirely withdraw from those Gentile nations, and leave them to themselves. Then they will find something else to do besides warring against the saints in their midst-besides raising their sword and fighting against the Lamb of God; for then war will commence in earnest, and such a war as probably never entered into the hearts of man in our age to conceive of. No nation of the Gentiles upon the face of the whole earth but what will be engaged in deadly war, except the latter-day kingdom. They will be fighting one against another. And when that day comes, the Jews will flee to Jerusalem, and those nations will almost use one another up, and those of them who are left will be burned for that will be the last sweeping judgment that is to go over the earth to cleanse it from wickedness. (Orson Pratt, JD 7:188.)

NEARNESS OF THE FULFILLMENT OF THE SIGNS OF THE TIMES

The servants of God will not have gone over the nations of the Gentiles, with a warning voice, until the destroying angel will commence to waste the inhabitants of the earth, and as the prophet hath said, "It shall be a vexation to hear the report." I speak thus because I feel for my fellow men; I do it in the name of the Lord, being moved upon by the Holy Spirit. Oh, that I could snatch them from the vortex of misery, into which I behold them plunging themselves, by their sins; that I might be enabled by the warning voice, to be an instrument of bringing them to unfeigned repentance, that they might have faith to stand in the evil day! (Joseph Smith, DPJS, 238.)

THE DAYS OF TRIBULATION ARE FAST APPROACHING

We have all been children, and are too much so at the present time; but we hope in the Lord that we may grow in grace and be prepared for all things which the bosom of futurity may disclose unto us. Time is rapidly rolling on, and the prophecies must be fulfilled. The days of tribulation are fast approaching, and the time to test the fidelity of the saints has come. Rumor with her ten thousand tongues is diffusing her uncertain sounds in almost every ear;

but in these times of sore trial, let the saints be patient and see the salvation of God. Those who cannot endure persecution, and stand in the day of affliction, cannot stand in the day when the Son of God shall burst the veil, and appear in all the glory of his Father, with all the holy angels. (Joseph Smith, DPJS, 239-240.)

EVENTS OF THE LAST DAYS

Comfort ye, comfort ye my people, saith your God.

Speak ye comfortably to Jerusalem, and cry unto her, that her warfare is accomplished, that her iniquity is pardoned; for she hath received of the Lord's hand double for all her sins.

The voice of him that crieth in the wilderness, Prepare ye the way of the Lord, make straight in the desert a highway for our God.

Every valley shall be exalted, and every mountain and hill shall be made low; and the crooked shalt be made straight, and the rough places plain:

And the glory of the Lord shall be revealed, and all flesh shall see it together; for the mouth of the Lord hath spoken it. (Isa. 40: 1-5.)

From these verses we learn, first, that the voice of one shall be heard in the wilderness, to prepare the way of the Lord, just at the time when Jerusalem has been trodden down of the Gentiles long enough to have received, at the Lord's hands, double for all her sins, yea, when the warfare of Jerusalem is accomplished, and her iniquities pardoned. Then shall this proclamation be made as it was before by John the Baptist, yea, a second proclamation, to prepare the way of the Lord, for his second coming, and about that time every valley shall be exalted, and every mountain and hill shall be made low, and crooked shall be made straight, and rough places plain, and then the glory of the Lord shall be revealed, and all flesh shall see it together, for the mouth of the Lord hath⎮spoken it....

Having restored the earth to the same glorious state in which it first existed-leveling the mountains, exalting the valleys, smoothing the rough places, making the deserts fruitful, and bringing all the continents and islands together, causing the curse to be taken off, that noxious weeds and thorns, and thistles shall no longer be produced-the next thing is to regulate and restore the brute creation to their former state of peace and glory, causing enmity to cease from off the earth. But this will never be done until there is a general destruction poured out upon man, which will entirely cleanse the earth, and sweep all wickedness from its face. (Parley P. Pratt, VW 95-97.)

MISSIONARIES TO BE CALLED HOME

All we have yet heard and we have experienced is scarcely a preface to the sermon that is going to be preached. When the testimony of the elders ceases to be given, and the Lord says to them, "Come home; I will now preach my own sermons to the nations of the earth," all you now know can scarcely be called a preface to the sermon that will be preached with fire and sword, tempests, earthquakes, hail, rain, thunders and lightnings, and fearful destruction. What matters the destruction of a few railway cars? You will hear of magnificent cities, now idolized by the people, sinking in the earth, entombing the inhabitants. The sea will heave itself beyond its bounds, engulfing mighty cities. Famine will spread over the nations and nation will rise up against nation, kingdom against kingdom and states against states, in our own country and in foreign lands; and they will destroy each other caring not for the blood and lives of their neighbors, of their families, or for their own lives. (Brigham Young, JD 8: 123.)

LAW

OBEY, HONOR, AND SUSTAIN THE LAW

The three significant words in the 12th Article of Faith express the proper attitude of the membership of the Church toward law. These words are-obey, honor, and sustain.

The Article does not say we believe in submission to the law. Obedience implies a higher attitude than mere submission, for obedience has its root in good intent; submission may spring from selfishness or meanness of spirit. Though obedience and submission both imply restraint on one's own will, we are obedient only from a sense of right; submissive from a sense of necessity.

Honor expresses an act or attitude of an inferior towards a superior. When applied to things it is taken in the sense of holding in honor. Thus, in honoring the law, we look upon it as something which is above selfish desires or indulgences.

To sustain signifies to hold up; to keep from falling. To sustain the law, therefore, is to refrain from saying or doing anything which will weaken it or make it ineffective.

We obey law from a sense of right.

We honor law because of its necessity and strength to society.

We sustain law by keeping it in good repute. (David O. McKay, CR April 1937, 28.)

IF ALL NATURE IS UNDER LAW, WHY NOT MAN?

According to the eternal laws of God and the eternal fitness of things as they exist with him in the eternal worlds and as they exist here upon the earth, all of us are... as much obligated to listen to his law and be governed by his counsels and advice... [as] we would be in making a grain of wheat to grow .... Being the God and the Father of the spirits of all flesh, and having made a world for all flesh to inhabit, and having made provision for the sustenance of that flesh, for their food, clothing, comfort, convenience and happiness, and having given them intelligence and told them to go forth and manipulate the abundance of nature to their use, has he not a right to lead and direct us, to ask obedience to his law? Would not that be a legitimate right, when we reflect upon it? The world says, No, he has no right; I am my own master, etc. Some of the Latter-day Saints almost say the same thing; not quite, but they would like to get near it. "I am a free man; I will be damned if I don't do as I please," etc. Well, I will tell you another part of that story. You will be damned if you do act as you please unless you please to do and to keep the laws of God. We cannot violate his laws with impunity nor trample under foot these eternal principles which exist in all nature. If all nature is compelled to be governed by law or suffer loss, why not man?

Now, then, he has revealed unto us the gospel. He has gathered us together from among the nations of the earth for the accomplishment of his purposes. For this he has used higher measures and more exalted principles than are associated with some of the lower orders of nature .... It is for us to learn this lesson and to find out that there is a God who rules in heaven, and that he manages, directs and controls the affairs of the human family. We are not our own rulers. We are all the children of God. He is our Father and has a right to direct us, not only us, but has a perfect right to direct and control the affairs of all the human family that exist upon the face of the earth for they are all his offspring. Now, he feels kindly towards them and knows what kind of people they are, and also what we are, and he would do everything he could for them even if in his almighty wisdom he has to kill them off in order to save them. He destroyed the antediluvian world on that account, because they were not filling the measure of their creation. They had corrupted themselves to such an extent that it would have been an injustice to the spirits in the eternal world if they had to come through such a corrupt lineage to be subject to all the trouble incident thereunto. And therefore God destroyed them. He cut off the cities of Sodom and Gomorrah in consequence of their corruptions, and by and by he will shake all the inhabitants of the earth, he will shake thrones and will overturn empires and desolate the land and lay millions of the human family in the dust. Plagues and pestilence will stalk through the earth because of the iniquities of men, because of some of these corruptions...namely, the perversion of the laws of nature between the sexes, and the damnable murders that exist among men. (John Taylor, JD 21:113-116.)

GOD GOVERNS BY LAW

If man has grown to wisdom and is capable of discerning the propriety of laws to govern nations, what less can be expected from the Ruler and Upholder of the universe? Can we suppose that he has a kingdom without laws? Or do we believe that it is composed of an innumerable company of beings who are entirely beyond all law? Consequently have need of nothing to govern or regulate them? Would not such ideas be a reproach to our Great Parent, and at variance with his glorious intelligence? Would it not be asserting that man had found out a secret beyond Deity? That he had learned that it was good to have laws, while God after existing from eternity and having power to create man, had not found out that it was proper to have laws for his government? We admit that God is the great source and fountain from whence proceeds all good; that he is perfect intelligence, and that his wisdom is alone sufficient to govern and regulate the mighty creations and worlds which shine and blaze with such magnificence and splendor over our heads, as though touched with his finger and moved by his Almighty word. And if so, it is done and regulated by law; for without law all must certainly fall into chaos. (Joseph Smith, DPJS, 285.)

LIFE

THE PRINCIPLE OF LIFE

There is a principle of life associated with the gospel-life temporal, life spiritual, and life eternal. Hence men are called to be fathers of lives, and women are called to be mothers of lives. We are fathers and mothers of lives. And there is something different associated with the order of God from any order of men that exists upon the earth.

When God created the earth and placed man upon it, and the fishes of the sea and the fowls of the air, and the grasses and plants and trees, etc., he placed in them the principle of life, or, in other words, the power of propagating their own species. And if it were not for that, what would you farmers do? Men can accomplish a great many things. They can build houses, railroads, and steamboats, and can do a great many clever things whereby they can command, to a certain extent, the forces of nature; but they cannot give vitality to any of them. They cannot even furnish material to make a grain of sand, the wisest of them. But God has ordained that this principle of vitality exists within themselves. You take a single grain of wheat, for instance, and put it into the earth and you will see the principle of life begin to manifest itself; it is very small apparently, but contains within itself the power of increase. The same is also true with regard to the grasses, shrubs, plants, and flowers, and the various things that exist in creation. They spread, they extend, and they have spread over the face of the earth as man has spread, and the rain descends and the sun shines and nature, as we term it, operates; but I would call it the power of God which operates according to eternal laws and principles that he has ordained. He gives vitality to all creation and sets life into motion and controls it, in the heavens as well as in the earth; not only among men, but among the beasts of the field, the fowls of the air, the fishes of the sea, and all the grasses, plants and flowers and herbs, etc., everything possessing the principle of life within itself ....

This principle of life is the origin of our world, not only of this world, but of others; and this propagating and multiplying is ordained of the Almighty for the peopling of' these worlds. And this production of life that I have briefly alluded to is another principle that exists to supply the want of another kind of life that exists here upon the earth. And without this there could be no world; all would be chaos, all would be darkness, all would be death, and the works of God would amount to nothing if it were not for this life and vitality. (John Taylor, JD 21:112-113.)

LIFE IS ETERNAL

All the learning and knowledge upon the face of the earth cannot, of themselves, make or produce a spear of grass, or the smallest leaf upon a tree. Do you know where they come from and what produces them? I know their origin and mode of production, and so do you, though you may not, in your reflections, have fully carried out the ideas connected with that subject. (Brigham Young, JD 3:276.)

LIFE IN ALL THINGS

Associated with matter-energy was the implication in Joseph Smith's teachings that the energy in the universe is a form of intelligence; that is, in a manner not fully understood by man, some form of life resides in all matter, though of an order wholly different from the organized intelligence of men or higher living things. Hence, everything in the universe is alive. The differences among rock, plant, beast, and man are due to the amount and organization of life element. Confirming this view, the Prophet in a revelation said: "Wherefore, it shall be sanctified; yea, notwithstanding it shall die, it shall be quickened again, and shall abide the power by which it is quickened, and the righteous shall inherit it."

That implies clearly that the earth is a living organism.

President Brigham Young who was trained in the gospel by the Prophet confirmed the teaching that life and intelligence 'pervade all things, animate and inanimate. "Are this earth, the air and the water composed of life?... We suggest that there is an eternity of organization, and an eternity of intelligence from the highest to the lowest grade, every creature in its order from the Gods to the animalculae." (The Resurrection, 1884 edition, p. 3.)

We live then in a living universe which in all its component parts is intelligent. (John A. Widtsoe, JS 149-150.)

DO NOT DESTROY LIFE WANTONLY

I have just a few words to say in addition to those that have already been said, in relation to shedding blood and to the destruction of life. I think that every soul should be impressed by the sentiments that have been expressed here this evening by all who have spoken, and not less with reference to the killing of our innocent birds, natives of our country, who live upon the vermin that are indeed enemies to the farmer and to mankind. It is not only wicked to destroy them, it is abominable, in my opinion. I think that this principle should extend, not only to the bird life, but to the life of all animals. When I visited, a few years ago, the Yellowstone National Park, and saw in the streams and the beautiful lakes, birds swimming quite fearless of man, allowing passersby to approach them as closely almost as tame birds, and apprehending no fear of them, and when I saw droves of beautiful deer herding along the side of the road, as fearless of the presence of men as any domestic animal, it filled my heart with a degree of peace and joy that seemed to be almost a foretaste of that period hoped for when there shall be none to hurt and none to molest in all the land, especially among all the inhabitants of Zion.

These same birds, if they were to visit other regions, inhabited by man, would, on account of their tameness, doubtless become more easily a prey to the gunner. The same may be said of those beautiful creatures-the deer and antelope. If they should wander out of the park, beyond the protection that is established there for these animals, they would become, of course, an easy prey to those who were seeking their lives. I never could see why a man should be imbued with a blood-thirsty desire to kill and destroy animal life. I have known men-and they still exist among us-who enjoy what is, to them, the "sport" of hunting birds and slaying them by the hundreds, and who will come in after a day's sport, boasting of how many harmless birds they have had the skill to slaughter, and day after day, during the season when it is lawful for men to hunt and kill (the birds having had a season of protection and not apprehending danger) go out by scores or hundreds; and you may hear their   guns early in the morning on
the day of the opening, as if great armies had met in battle; and the terrible work of slaughtering the innocent birds goes on.

I do not believe any man should kill animals or birds unless he needs them for food, and then he should not kill innocent birds that are not intended for food for man. I think it is wicked for men to thirst in their souls to kill almost everything which possesses animal life. It is wrong, and I have been surprised at prominent men whom I have seen whose very souls seemed to be athirst for the shedding of animal blood. They go off hunting deer, antelope, elk, anything they can find, and what for? "Just for the fun of it!" Not that they are hungry and need the flesh of their prey, but just because they love to shoot and destroy life. I am a firm believer, with reference to these things, in the simple words of one of the poets:

> Take not away the life you cannot give.
> For all things have an equal right to live.

(Joseph F. Smith, JI 48:308-309.)

LOVE

LOVE, A CHIEF CHARACTERISTIC OF DEITY

Love is one of the chief characteristics of Deity, and ought to be manifested by those who aspire to be the sons of God. A man filled with the love of God is not content with blessing his family alone, but ranges through the whole world, anxious to bless the whole human race. (Joseph Smith, DPJS, 205.)

WE SHOULD PUT LOVE OF GOD AND HIS WORK ABOVE ALL ELSE

When we lose a near and dear friend, upon whom we have set our hearts, it should be a caution unto us not to set our affections too firmly upon others, knowing that they may in like manner be taken from us. Our affections should be placed upon God and his work, more intensely than upon our fellow beings. (Joseph Smith, DPJS, 205.)

THE PRINCIPLE OF LOVE

Joseph remarked that all was well between him and the heavens; that he had no enmity against anyone; and as the prayer of Jesus, or his pattern, so prayed Joseph–"Father, forgive me my trespasses as I forgive those who trespass against me," for I freely forgive all men. If we would secure and cultivate-the love of others, we must love others, even our enemies as well as friends.
Sectarian priests cry out concerning me, and ask, "Why is it this babbler gains so many followers, and retains them?" I answer, It is because I possess the principle of love. All I can offer the world is a good heart and a good hand.

The saints can testify whether I am willing to lay down my life for my brethren. If it has been demonstrated that I have been willing to die for a "Mormon," I am bold to declare before heaven that I am just as ready to die in defending the rights of a Presbyterian, a Baptist, or a good man of any other denomination; for the same principle which would trample upon the rights of the Latter-day Saints would trample upon the rights of the Roman Catholics, or of any other denomination who may be unpopular and too weak to defend themselves.

It is a love of liberty which inspires my soul-civil and religious liberty to the whole of the human race. Love of liberty was diffused into my soul by my grandfathers while they dandled me on their knees. (Joseph Smith, DPJS, 206.)

THE POWER OF LOVE

Nothing is so much calculated to lead people to forsake sin as to take them by the hand, and watch over them with tenderness. When persons manifest the least kindness and love to me, O what power it has over my mind, while the opposite course has a tendency to harrow up all the harsh feelings and depress the human mind. (Joseph Smith, DPJS, 208-209.)

LET US LOVE ONE ANOTHER

I say there is need in all Israel today-there is need for this man addressing you to examine himself-there is need for everyone of us to look about ourselves and see wherein we are neglecting our privileges and our duty, for tomorrow it may be too late. Today is the acceptable time of the Lord. Let us set our houses in order. Let us love one another. Let us sustain these men whom God has raised up to preside over us. Let us bless them, not only by our lips, but by assisting in every possible way to carry this burden that rests so heavily upon their shoulders. Let us honor these presidents of stakes and these bishops of wards; pray for and bless them and help them. Let us love one another that our Heavenly Father may be able to bless us, and he will bless us if we love one another and do good to all his children. (George Albert Smith, CR October 1930, 69.)

LOVE ONE ANOTHER

Talking about people giving away to passion and giving expression to hard words-such things do not belong to the gospel, to no part of it. They come from beneath. I hear a man say sometimes, "I hate such a man." Why, I do not know of a person that I hate in the world. The command is to love one another. When Jesus was about to leave his disciples, the burden of his prayer was, "Father, I pray for these whom thou hast given me; thine they were, and thou gavest them me. I pray for them, Father, that they may be one, even as I and thou art one, that they may be one in us." (Compare John 17:20-23.) What, a sister or brother, a citizen of the kingdom of God, a member of The Church of Jesus Christ of Latter-day Saints, one who has received peradventure of the ordinances of the house of God, and who expects to associate with the saints of God, quarrels with his brother about peanuts and baby toys and then talk about your honor being infringed upon! I tell you if you take care of yourself, your honor will take care of itself and you need not be concerned about it.

Treat one another aright. Have you sinned against another? Then go and make restitution. Have you defrauded one another? Go and make it right. Have you spoken unkindly to your brother or sister? Then go and acknowledge your wrong and ask to be forgiven, promising to do better in the future. And then he or she might say, on the other hand, "Yes, and I said so and so the other day, won't you please forgive me?" How much better and how much more in keeping with the calling of a saint of God such a course would be than to harbor hard feelings in the heart. (John Taylor, JD 21:98-99.)

THE BLESSING OF HAVING PERFECT LOVE

Until we have perfect love we are liable to fall and when we have a testimony that our names are sealed in the Lamb's book of life we have perfect love and then it is impossible for false Christs to deceive us. (Joseph Smith, Far West Record 16.)

FRIENDSHIP AND LOVE UNITE THE HUMAN FAMILY

Friendship is one of the grand fundamental principles of "Mormonism"; [it is designed] to revolutionize and civilize the world, and cause wars and contentions to cease and men to become friends and brothers. Even the wolf and the lamb shall dwell together; the leopard shall lie down with the kid, the calf, the young lion and the fatling; and a little child shall lead them; the bear and the cow shall lie down together, and the sucking child shall play on the hole of the asp, and the weaned child shall play on the cockatrice's den; and they shall not hurt or destroy in all my holy mountains, saith the Lord of Hosts. (Isaiah.)

It is a time-honored adage that love begets love. Let us pour forth love-show forth our kindness unto all mankind, and the Lord will reward us with everlasting increase; cast our bread upon the waters and we shall receive it after many days, increased to a 'hundredfold. Friendship is like Brother Turley in his blacksmith shop welding iron to iron; it unites the human family with its happy influence. (Joseph Smith, DPJS, 205.)

A MESSAGE OF LOVE

The restored gospel is a message of divine love for all people everywhere, based upon the conviction that all humans are children of the same God.

....Latter-day Saints have a positive and inclusive approach toward others who are not of our faith. We believe they are literally our brothers and sisters, that we are sons and daughters of the same Heavenly Father. We have a common genealogy leading back to God. But more than that, we also seek the true and the beautiful wherever it may be found. And we know that God has blessed all his children with goodness and light, in accordance with the conditions in which they find themselves. (Howard W. Hunter, ES, May 1991, 19).

MAN

MAN IS NATURALLY GOOD

It is true mankind have wandered and have fallen from that which they might have attained through the redemption made by Jesus Christ; but there is one point in connection with this statement on which I differ from the orthodox divines of the day. They say that man is naturally prone to evil. In some respects this is true, whereby the force of example and wrong tradition has become ingrained, but if man had always been permitted to follow the instincts of his nature, had he always followed the great and holy principles of his organism, they would have led him into the path of life everlasting, which the whole human family are constantly trying to find. (Brigham Young, JD 10:189.)

MAN IS INCLINED TO DO RIGHT

Many of us have been taught the doctrine of total depravity that man is not naturally inclined to do good. I am satisfied that he is more inclined to do right than to do wrong. There is a greater power within him to shun evil and perform good, than to do the opposite. (Brigham Young, JD 9:247.)

MAN IS THE OFFSPRING OF GOD

If we take man, he is said to have been made in the image of God, for the simple reason that he is a son of God, and being his son, he is, of course, his offspring, an emanation from God, in whose likeness, we are told, he is made. He did not originate from a chaotic mass of matter, moving or inert, but came forth Possessing, in an embryonic state, all the faculties and powers of a God. And when he shall be perfected, and have progressed to maturity, he will be like his Father-a God, being indeed his off-spring. As the horse, the ox, the sheep, and every living creature, including man, propagates its own species and perpetuates its own kind, so does God perpetuate his. (John Taylor, MA 164-165.)

MAN'S RELATIONSHIP TO GOD

A man, as a man, could arrive at all the dignity that a man was capable of obtaining or receiving; but it needed a God to raise him to the dignity of a God. (John Taylor, MA 145.)

MAN IS HIS OWN TORMENTOR AND CONDEMNER

A man is his own tormentor and his own condemner. Hence the saying, They shall go into the lake that burns with fire and brimstone. The torment of disappointment in the mind of man is as exquisite as a lake burning with fire and brimstone. I say, so is the torment of man. (Joseph Smith, DPJS, 132.)

MEN MAY BECOME GODS

Man is made an agent to himself before his God; he is organized for the express purpose that he may become like his Master
....
The Lord created you and me for the purpose of becoming gods like himself; when we have been proved in our present capacity and have been faithful with all things he puts into our possession. We are created, we are born for the express purpose of Vowing up

from the low estate of manhood, to become gods like unto our Father in heaven. That is the truth about it, just as it is. The Lord has organized mankind for the express purpose of increasing in that intelligence and truth, which is with God, until he is capable of creating worlds on worlds, and becoming gods, even the sons of God. (Brigham Young, JD 3:93.)

COUNSEL WITH WISE MEN

The way to get along in any important matter is to gather unto yourselves wise men, experienced and aged men, to assist in council in all times of trouble. Handsome men are not apt to be wise and strong-minded men; but the strength of a strong-minded man will generally create coarse features, like the rough, strong bough of the oak. You will always discover in the first glance of a man, in the outlines of his features something of his mind. (Joseph Smith, DPJS, 211.)

MARRIAGE

A MARRIAGE CAN BE ONE OF PEACE

"A marriage may not always be even or incidentless, but it can be one of great peace. A couple may have poverty, illness, disappointment, failures, and even death in the family, but even these will not rob them of their peace. The marriage can be successful so long as selfishness does not enter in. Troubles and problems will draw parents together into unbreakable unions if there is total unselfishness there." (Spencer W. Kimball, Marriage and Divorce, Salt Lake City: Deseret Book Co., 1976, p. 17.)

LEGITIMACY OF ETERNAL MARRIAGE EXPLAINED

Why is a woman sealed to a man for time and all eternity? Because there is legitimate power on earth to do it. This power will bind on earth and in heaven. It can loose on earth, and it is loosed in heaven. It can seal on earth, and it is sealed in heaven. There is a legitimate, authorized agent of God upon earth. This sealing power is regulated by him. Hence what is done by that, is done right, and is recorded. When the books are opened, every one will find his proper mate, and have those that belong to him, and every one will be deprived of that which is surreptitiously obtained. (John Taylor, JD 1:232.)

THE EXTENT OF THE MARRIAGE RELATION

But the whole subject of the marriage relation is not in my reach, nor in any other man's reach on this earth. It is without beginning of days or end of years; it is a hard matter to reach. We can tell some things with regard to it; it lays the foundation for worlds, for angels, and for the gods; for intelligent beings to be crowned with glory, immortality, and eternal lives. In fact, it is the thread which runs from the beginning to the end of the holy gospel of salvation-of the gospel of the Son of God; it is from eternity to eternity. (Brigham Young, JD 2:90.)

THE FIRST MARRIAGE

The first marriage on record appertaining to this earth was solemnized by the Almighty. The first couple married were immortal beings-Adam and Eve, our first parents-before they had partaken of the forbidden fruit and became subject to the penalty of death-Marriage, as then understood, could not have been what it is now popularly supposed to be by the so-called Christian word. Then the marriage vow was made and the ceremony was performed by immortal or celestial beings, with no reference to death or to a time when that sacred and holy union should cease. (Joseph F. Smith, MS 36:312.)

THE LAW OF CELESTIAL MARRIAGE

The Lord has revealed unto us the ancient law, which was revealed to Adam through the gospel and which is called the law i Of celestial marriage. This... applies only to certain conditions of men and can only be enjoyed by parties who have obeyed the everlasting gospel. It is one of the eternal principles associated therewith, uniting mortal and immortal beings by eternal covenants, that will live and endure forever .... But with regard to the law of celestial marriage, there are certain safeguards thrown around it, as there always were, and those safeguards are, and always were, in the hands of the proper authorities and priesthood, delegated by God to man for the protection and preservation and right use of this most important, sacred, exalting and eternal ceremony or covenant. These things are clearly defined in the revelation on celestial marriage and can rightly only be enjoyed and participated in by such as are considered worthy, according to the laws, rites, privileges and immunities connected therewith.... Are the barriers placed around this sacred institution to be broken down and trampled underfoot? And are unworthy characters who do not fulfill the requirements of the gospel to have conferred upon them the blessings of eternal lives, of thrones, and powers, and principalities in the celestial kingdom of God? We emphatically answer, No! (John Taylor, "On Marriage," 5-6, Published 1882.)

SISTERS, SELECT A MAN OF GOD

How is it with you, sisters? Do you distinguish between a man of God and a man of the world? It is one of the strangest things that happens in my existence, to think that any man or woman can love a being that will not receive the truth of heaven. The love this gospel produces is far above the love of women; it is the love of God-the love of eternity-of eternal lives. (Brigham Young, JD 8:199-200.)

YOUTH SHOULD MAKE EVERY EFFORT TO HAVE A TEMPLE MARRIAGE

I believe that no worthy young Latter-day Saint man or woman should spare any reasonable effort to come to a house of the Lord to begin life together. The marriage vows taken in these hallowed places and the sacred covenants entered into for time and all eternity are proof against many of the temptations of life that tend to break homes and destroy happiness....

The blessings and promises that come from beginning life together, for time and eternity, in a temple of the Lord, cannot be obtained in any other way and worthy young Latter-day Saint men and women who so begin life together find that their eternal partnership under the everlasting covenant becomes the foundation upon which are built peace, happiness, virtue, love, and all of the other eternal verities of life, here and hereafter. (Heber J. Grant, IE 39:198-199.)

TEMPLE MARRIAGE REACHES INTO ETERNITY

When two Latter-day Saints are united together in marriage, promises are made to them concerning their offspring that reach from eternity to eternity. They are promised that they shall have the power and the right to govern and control and administer salvation and exaltation and glory to their offspring worlds without end. And what offspring they do not have here, undoubtedly there will be opportunities to have them hereafter. What else could man wish? A man and a woman in the other life, having celestial bodies, free from sickness and disease, glorified and beautified beyond description, standing in the midst of their posterity, governing and controlling them, administering life, exaltation and glory, worlds without end. (Lorenzo Snow, DW 54:481 .) heirs with Jesus Christ. (Joseph F. Smith, GD 346-347.)

WHEN A WOMAN IS SEALED TO A MAN

When a woman is sealed to a man holding the priesthood, she becomes one with him....The glory and power and dominion that he will exercise when he has the fullness of the priesthood and becomes a "king and a priest unto God," she will share with him. Sisters have said to me sometimes, "But, I hold the priesthood with my husband." "Well," I asked, "what office do you hold in the priesthood?" Then they could not say much more. The sisters are not ordained to any office in the priesthood and there is authority in the Church which they cannot exercise; it does not belong to them; they cannot do that properly any more than they can change themselves into a man.... When you are sealed to a man of God who holds it [the priesthood] and who, by overcoming, inherits the fullness of the glory of God, you will share that with him if you are fit for it. (Charles W. Penrose, CR April 1921, 24.)

MILLENNIUM

EARTH CHANGES YET TO COME

In the resurrection which now approaches, and in connection with the glorious coming of Jesus Christ, the earth will undergo a change in its physical features, climate, soil, productions, and in its political, moral and spiritual government.

Its mountains will be leveled, its valleys exalted, its swamps and sickly places will be drained and become healthy, while its burning deserts and its frigid polar regions will be redeemed and become temperate and fruitful. (Parley P. Pratt, KT 139-140.)

EVERY KNEE SHALL BOW

In the millennium men will have the privilege of being Presbyterians, Methodists or infidels, but they will not have the privilege of treating the name and character of Deity as they have done heretofore. No, but every knee shall bow and every tongue confess to the glory of God the Father that Jesus is the Christ. (Brigham Young, JD 12:274.)

A THOUSAND YEARS' REST

There will be a thousand years' rest, during which period Satan will be bound, and when the seed of the righteous will increase and cover' the land. In that glorious period everything on the face of the earth will be beautiful; disease and crime, and all the evils that attend our present state of existence will be banished; and during that period, as God has revealed, the occupation of his people will be to lay a foundation for the redemption of the dead,' the unnumbered millions who lived and died on the earth without hearing and obeying the plan of salvation. (George Q. Cannon, JD 14:321-322.)

PREPARATION FOR THE MILLENNIUM

During the journey [Zion's Camp], when brethren would have killed the serpents which at times came into the tents and coiled up near the beds, the Prophet taught his brethren the beautiful principle that men themselves must become harmless before they can expect the brute creation to be so. When a man shall lose his own vicious disposition and cease to destroy the inferior animals, the lion and the lamb may dwell together, and the suckling child play with the serpent in safety. (Wilford Woodruff, WW 43.)

THE WORK TO BE DONE IN THE MILLENNIUM

In the millennium, when the kingdom of God is established on the earth in power, glory and perfection, and the reign of wickedness that has so long prevailed is subdued, the saints of God will have the privilege of building their temples, and of entering into them, becoming, as it were, pillars in the temples of God, and they will officiate for their dead. Then we will see our friends come up, and perhaps some that we have been acquainted with here. If we ask who will stand at the head of the resurrection in this last dispensation, the answer is-Joseph Smith, Junior, the Prophet of God. He is the man who will be resurrected and receive the keys of the resurrection, and he will seal this authority upon others, and they will hunt up their friends and resurrect them when they shall have been officiated for, and bring them up. And we will have revelations to know our forefathers clear back to Father Adam and

Mother Eve, and we will enter into the temples of God and officiate for them. Then man will be sealed to man until the chain is made perfect back to Adam, so that there will be a perfect chain of priesthood from Adam to the winding-up scene.

This will be the work of the Latter-day Saints in the millennium. (Brigham Young, JD 15:138-139.)

THE MILLENNIUM AND REDEMPTION OF THE DEAD

The great work of the millennium shall be the work in the temples for the redemption of the dead; and then we hope to enjoy the benefits of revelation through the Urim and Thummim, or by such means as the Lord may reveal concerning those for whom the work shall be done, so that we may not work by chance, or by faith alone, without knowledge, but with the actual knowledge revealed unto us. (Joseph F. Smith, IE 5:146-147.)

THE LORD WILL REIGN IN THE MILLENNIUM

The world has had a fair trial for six thousand years; the Lord will try the seventh thousand himself .... Satan will be bound, and the works of darkness destroyed; righteousness will be put to the line and judgment to the plummet, and "he that fears the Lord will alone be exalted in that day." (Joseph Smith, DPJS, 363.)

CHRIST AND THE RESURRECTED SAINTS DURING THE MILLENNIUM

I said, Christ and the resurrected saints will reign over the earth during the thousand years. They will not probably dwell upon the earth, but will visit it when they please, or when it is necessary to govern it. There will be wicked men on the earth during the thousand years. The heathen nations who will not come up to worship will be visited with the judgments of God, and must eventually be destroyed from the earth. (Joseph Smith, DPJS, 160.)

MIRACLES

MIRACLES AND THE SAVIOR

It is natural for me to believe that, if I plough the ground and sow wheat, in the proper season I shall reap a crop of wheat; this is the natural result. It was precisely so with the miracles that Jesus wrought upon the earth. At the wedding in Cana of Galilee, when they had drunk all the wine, they went to the Savior and asked him what they should do. He ordered them to fill up their pots with water, and after having done so they drew forth of that water and found that it was wine. I believe that was real wine; I do not believe that it was done on the principle that such things are done in these days by wicked men, who, by means of what they term psychology, electrobiology, mesmerism, etc., influence men and make them believe that water is wine, and other things of a similar character. The Savior converted the water into wine. He knew how to call the necessary elements together in order to fill the water with the properties of wine. The elements are all around us; we eat, drink and breathe them, and Jesus, understanding the process of calling them together, performed no miracle except to those who were ignorant of that process.

It was the same with the woman who was healed by touching the hem of his garment; she was healed by faith, but it was no miracle to Jesus. He understood the process, and although he was pressed by the crowd, behind and before, and on each side, so that he could scarcely make his way through it, the moment she touched him he felt virtue leave him and enquired who touched him. This was no miracle to him. He has the issues of life and death in his power; he had power to lay down his life and power to take it up again. This is what he says, and we must believe this if we believe the history of the Savior and the sayings of the apostles recorded in the New Testament. Jesus had this power in and of himself; the Father bequeathed 'it to him; it was his legacy, and he had the power to lay down his life and take it again. He had the streams and issues of life within him and when he said "Live" to individuals, they lived. The diseases that are and ever have been prevalent among the human family are from beneath, and are entailed upon them through the fall-through the disobedience of our first parents; but Jesus, having the issues of life at his command, could counteract those diseases at his pleasure.' The case of the centurion's servant is a striking instance of this. The centurion sent and besought Jesus to heal his servant. "Say in a word," said he, "and my servant shall be healed." Jesus, seeing the man's earnestness and solicitude, said, "I have not found so great faith, no, not in Israel." And it is said that they who were sent, returned to the centurion's house and found the servant healed. Jesus counteracted the disease preying upon the system of this man, but to himself knowing the principle by which the disease was rebuked, it was no miracle. (Brigham Young, JD 13:140-141.)

MIRACLES IN EVERYDAY LIFE

Today we can talk of railroads and steamboats. I remember the time, and many of you old people also remember, when there were no such things in existence. Well, but did not steam possess the same properties five thousand years ago as it does today? Yes, it did. The properties were precisely the same, but we did not understand it, that's all. The principles were the same, and there is an eternal law by which all these things are governed. The same thing applies to electricity. You remember very well when it took several months to send a message to Washington and receive an answer. Now we can do it in as many minutes. But did not that principle always exist? Yes; but man did not know how to avail himself of it. I remember the time too, very well, when there was no such thing as gas, when whale oil was used which produced a light that just about made darkness visible. We knew nothing about kerosene, or gasoline, or gas or any of these superior artificial lights. But the principles existed then as they do now, but we did not understand them. We did not comprehend the position of things and it is only quite recently that some of these discoveries have been brought into operation. The art of photography has not been long known. When I was a boy people would have laughed at you if you had talked of taking a man's likeness in a minute's time; yet it is done. Did not light always possess the same properties? Yes, but man did not understand it. The same thing applies to the mineral world, the vegetable kingdom, the animal creation, and all the works of God. They are all governed by certain laws. The vegetables which you grow here, how were they organized? God organized them and placed them upon the earth, and gave them power to propagate their species. So also with regard to the animal creation, as well as birds, fishes, insects, etc. (John Taylor, JD 20:130-131.)

MIRACLES ARE THE FRUITS OF FAITH

They who doubt the possibility of miracles are indeed without the power to perform them. But this does not prove that believers lack that power. Miracles are the fruits of faith-"These signs shall follow them that believe." The gist of the matter is this: These doubters have done away with God, or have tried to do away with him, and consequently are unable to conceive of a higher power than they themselves possess ....

Miracles are extraordinary results flowing from superior means and methods of doing things. When a man wants light he strikes a match, or presses a button, or turns a switch, and lo! there is light. When God wants light, he says: "Let there be light." It is simply a matter of knowing how to do things in a superior way, and having the power to do them. Man is gradually acquiring this power. It is a far call from the tallow dip to the electric light. But the end is not yet. Improvements will continue to be made, and some day, perhaps men may be able to make light just as the Lord makes it. Paradoxically, it might be said that the time will come when miracles will be so common that there will be none.

The Latter-day Saints are not strangers to the miraculous workings of divine power. Our history as a people is replete with such occurrences. I could relate many experiences of my own in support of this assertion, and so could these, my brethren, seated here upon the stand ....

Some years ago I was engaged to deliver a lecture in one of the towns south of this city, and was on my way to the lecture hall when I received a message from the bishop of the ward, asking me to come and administer to his little daughter, who was critically ill. Her doctor had said that she could not live till morning. Taking with me another elder, I proceeded to the bishop's home and we administered to the dying girl. Next morning a telephone message informed me that a marvelous change had taken place. The young patient, who had not slept for days prior to being blessed by us, immediately thereafter had sunk into a sweet and refreshing slumber. She slept twelve hours, and woke up normal, and continued so. The doctor was astounded, and the parents, of course, were overjoyed. The girl, then fifteen years of age, and now twenty-four, is an active member of the ward in which she resides, has a good position and goes to and from her work as well and as happy as if she had never known a day's illness.

Her physician had said that she could not live till morning and no doubt he was right, from his viewpoint. Medical science had so decreed, and but for the interposition of Divine Providence, that decree would probably have gone into effect. According to the lesser law, she should not live. But a greater law said: "She shall live." And the lesser could not operate in the presence of the greater.

Miracles belong to no particular time or place. Wherever and whenever there is a legitimate demand for the exercise of divine power, that power will act, and marvels will result. We worship a God of miracles, and he changeth not, but is the same yesterday, today and forever. There is but one valid reason for the absence of miracles among any people, and that is the absence of faith. "All things are possible to them that believe." (Orson F. Whitney, CR April 1925, 20-22.)

EVIL PERSONS REQUIRE MIRACLES

The gospel plan is so devised, that a miracle to make people believe would only be a condemnation to them. When you hear people tell what they have seen-that they have seen great and powerful miracles wrought, and they could not help believing remember that "devils believe and tremble," because they cannot help it. When the voice of the Good Shepherd is heard, the honest in heart believe and receive it. It is good to taste with the inward taste, to see with the inward eyes, and to enjoy with the sensations of the ever-living spirit. No person, unless he is an adulterer, a fornicator, covetous, or an idolater, will ever require a miracle; in other words, no good, honest person ever will. (Brigham Young, JD 8:42.)

MISSIONARY WORK

RESPONSIBILITY OF MISSIONARIES TO PREACH JESUS CHRIST

Preach Jesus Christ and him crucified; not to contend with others on account of their faith, or systems of religion, but pursue a steady course. This I delivered by way of commandment; and all who observe it not, will pull down persecution upon their heads, while those who do, shall always be filled with the Holy Ghost; this I pronounced as a prophecy, and sealed with hosanna and amen. (Joseph Smith, DPJS, 172.)

ELDERS TO PREACH REPENTANCE

Oh, ye elders of Israel, harken to my voice; and when you are sent into the world to preach, tell those things you are sent to tell; preach and cry aloud, "Repent ye, for the kingdom of heaven is at hand; repent and believe the Gospel." Declare the first principles, and let mysteries alone, lest ye be overthrown. Never meddle with the visions of beasts and subjects you do not understand. Elder Brown, when you go to Palmyra, say nothing about the four beasts, but preach those things the Lord has told you to preach about-repentance and baptism for the remission of sins. (Joseph Smith, DPJS, 172.)

THE MISSION FIELD IS THE WORLD

Take Jacob Zundell and Frederick H. Moeser... and send them to Germany; and when you meet with an Arab, send him to Arabia; when you find an Italian, send him to Italy; and a Frenchman, to France; or an Indian, that is suitable, send him among the Indians. Send them to the different places where they belong. Send somebody to Central America and to all Spanish America; and don't let a single corner of the earth go without a mission. (Joseph Smith, DPJS, 173.)

IMPORTANCE OF CHARACTER TO MISSIONARIES

But the most important standard is character. Let each one whom you interview sense the fact that he is going out as a representative. Some of the brethren have urged that each ward should have in the mission field a certain percentage of the ward membership. That is not an ideal. If you have no one who is worthy and financially able to represent the Church, do not send anybody out, but sit down with these young men and women and say, "If you accept this call willingly, you go out as a trusted representative of the Church an4 of the Lord Jesus Christ." And to be trusted, young men, is a greater compliment than to be loved, and you cannot violate that trust. You are obligated to keep that trust between now and the time you go to the missionary home. Maintain the Church standards with your companions who will want to give you a farewell party. We have heard of some missionaries who have been called who have joined in with their fraternity friends in actions that reflected discredit upon themselves and upon the missionary cause.

Tell the young man, "From now on, from this very moment, you are a trusted representative of this ward, of your parents, and of the Lord Jesus Christ." (David O. McKay, CR April 1950, 176-178.)

MISSIONARIES GO FORTH IN THE NAME OF ISRAEL'S GOD

When men go forth in the name of Israel's God, there is no power on earth that can overturn the truths they advocate. Men may misrepresent and calumniate them; they may circulate false reports, for as a general thing men love lies better than truth; but when men go forth possessing the truths of the everlasting gospel which God has revealed, they have a treasure within them that the world knows nothing about. They have the light of revelation, the fire of the Holy Ghost, and the power of the priesthood within them-a power that they know very little about even themselves, which, like a wellspring of life, is rising, bursting, bubbling, and spreading its exhilarating streams around. Why, says the Lord, with you I will confound the nations of the earth, with you I will overturn their kingdoms. (John Taylor, JD 12:396-397.)

MISSIONARY WORK

"The scriptures are replete with commands and promises and calls and rewards for teaching the gospel. I use the word command deliberately for it seems to be an insistent directive from which we, singly and collectively, cannot escape....

"It seems to me that the Lord chose his words when he said 'every nation,' 'every land,' 'uttermost bounds of the earth,' 'every tongue,' 'every people,' 'every soul,' 'all the world,' 'many lands.'

"Surely there is significance. in these words!", (Spencer W. Kimball, ES, Oct. 1974, pp. 4-5.)

PRAY FOR MISSIONARY WORK

"I'm hoping that, beginning now, the prayers of the Saints will be greatly increased from what they have been in the past, that we will never think of praying except we pray for the Lord to establish his program and make it possible that we can carry the gospel to his people as he has commanded. It is my deep interest and great prayer to you that this will be accomplished." (Spencer W. Kimball, ES, Nov. 1978, p. 46.)

WOMEN AND MISSIONARY SERVICE

It is surprising how eagerly the young women and some married women seek calls to go on missions. We commend them for it, but the responsibility of proclaiming the gospel of Jesus Christ rests primarily upon the priesthood of the Church.

In this connection, we advise that mothers who have dependent children, that means children who are in their teens or unmarried, should not be called on missions even though the grandparents are willing to take care of the children. No nobler work in this world can be performed by any mother than to rear and love the children with whom God has blessed her. That is her duty, and that is far greater than going out into the world to proclaim the gospel because somebody else can do that who does not bear the responsibility of rearing and loving the children who call her mother. (David O. McKay, CR April 1951, 81.)

OUR MISSION IS TO PREACH THE GOSPEL

I repeat, our mission is to preach the gospel, and then to gather the people who embrace it. And why? That there might be a nucleus formed, a people gathered who would be under the inspiration of the Almighty, and who would be willing to listen to the voice of God, a people who would receive and obey his word when it was made known to them. And this people in their gathered condition are called Zion, or the pure in heart. (John Taylor, JD 23:262.)

MORMONISM

MORMONISM EMBRACES EVERY PRINCIPLE

"Mormonism," so-called, embraces every principle pertaining to life and salvation, for time and eternity. No matter who has it. If the infidel has got truth it belongs to "Mormonism." The truth and sound doctrine possessed by the sectarian world, and they have a great deal, all belongs to this Church. As for their morality, many of them are, morally, just as good as we are. All that is good, lovely, and praiseworthy belongs to this Church and kingdom. "Mormonism" includes all truth. There is no truth but what belongs to the Gospel. It is life, eternal life; it is bliss; it is the fullness of all things in the gods and in the eternities of the gods. (Brigham Young, JD 11:375.)

THE COMPREHENSIVE NATURE OF MORMONISM

Is there a true principle of science in the world? It is ours. Are there true principles of music, or mechanism, or of philosophy? If there are, they are all ours. Is there a true principle of government that exists in the world anywhere? It is ours, it is God's; for every good and perfect gift that does exist in the world among men proceeds from the "Father of lights with whom there is no variableness, neither shadow of turning." It is God that has given every good gift that the world ever did possess. He is the giver of all good principles-of law, of government, and of everything else-and he is now gathering them together into one place, and withdrawing them from the world, and hence the misery and darkness that begin to prevail among the nations; and hence the light, life, and intelligence that begin to manifest themselves among us. (John Taylor, JD 10:57.)

MORMONISM WILL PREVAIL

When the wicked have power to blow out the sun, that it shines no more; when they have power to bring to a conclusion the operations of the elements, suspend the whole system of nature, and make a footstool of the throne of the Almighty, they may then think to check "Mormonism" in its course, and thwart the unalterable purposes of heaven. Men may persecute the people who believe its doctrines, report and publish lies to bring tribulation upon their heads, earth and hell may unite in one grand league against it, and exert their malicious powers to the utmost, but it will stand as firm and immovable in the midst of it all as the pillars of eternity. Men may persecute the Prophet, and those who believe and uphold him, they may drive the saints and kill them, but this does not affect the truths of "Mormonism" one iota, for they will stand when the elements melt with fervent heat, and the heavens are wrapped up like a scroll, and the solid earth is dissolved. "Mormonism" stands upon the eternal basis of omnipotence. Jehovah is the "Mormonism" of this people, their priesthood and their power; and all who adhere to it will, in the appointed day, come up into the presence of the King Eternal, and receive a crown of life. (Brigham Young, JD 1:88.)

THE ENIGMA OF MORMONISM

Mormonism is an enigma to the world .... Philosophy cannot comprehend it; it is beyond the reach of natural philosophy. It is the philosophy of heaven; it is the revelation of God to man. It is philosophical, but it is heavenly philosophy, and beyond the ken of human judgment, beyond the reach of human intelligence. They cannot grasp it; it is as high as heaven; what can they know about it? It is deeper than hell; they cannot fathom it. It is as wide as the universe; it extends over. all creation. It goes back into eternity and forward into eternity. It is associated with the past, present, and future. It is connected with time and eternity, with men, angels, and Gods, with beings that were, that are, and that are to come. (John Taylor, JD 15:25.)

MORTALITY

FAITHFULNESS DETERMINED OUR ESTATE HERE
We have been placed upon this earth because of our faithfulness in having kept our first estate. The labors that we performed in the sphere that we left before we came here have had a certain effect upon our lives here, and to a certain extent they govern and control the lives that we lead here, just the same as the labors that we do here will control and govern our lives when we pass from this stage of existence. (Heber J. Grant, IE 46:75.)

TRIALS AND EXPERIENCES NECESSARY IN MORTALITY
All intelligent beings who are crowned with crowns of glory, immortality, and eternal lives must pass through every ordeal appointed for intelligent beings to pass through, to gain their glory and exaltation. Every calamity that can come upon mortal beings will be suffered to come upon the few, to prepare them to enjoy the presence of the Lord. If we obtain the glory that Abraham obtained, we must do so by the same means that he did... we must pass through the same experience and gain the knowledge, intelligence, and endowments that will prepare us to enter into the celestial kingdom of our Father and God... Every trial and experience you have passed through is necessary for your salvation. (Brigham Young, JD 8:150.)

WE MUST PREPARE OURSELVES WHILE ON EARTH
The object of our being placed upon this earth is that we may work out an exaltation, that we may prepare ourselves to go back and dwell with our Heavenly Father; and our Father, knowing the faults and failings of men, has given us certain commandments to

obey, and if we will examine those requirements and the things that devolve upon us we will find that they are all for our individual benefit and advancement. The school of life in which we are placed and the lessons that are given to us by our Father will make of us exactly what he desires, so that we may be prepared to dwell with him. (Heber J. Grant, IE 48:123.)

GOD'S GOSPEL LAW INSURES HAPPINESS

[God] never has-he never will institute an ordinance or give a commandment to his people that is not calculated in its nature to promote that happiness which he has designed, and which will not end in the greatest amount of good and glory to those who become the recipients of his law and ordinances. (Joseph Smith, HC 5:135-136.)

MURDERERS

MURDERERS CANNOT BE FORGIVEN UNTIL THEY HAVE PAID THE "LAST FARTHING"

'Peter preached repentance and baptism for the remission of sins to the Jews who had been led to acts of violence and blood by their leaders; but to the rulers he said, "I would that through ignorance ye did it, as did also those ye ruled." "Repent, therefore, and be converted, that your sins may be blotted out, when the times of refreshing (redemption) shall come from the presence of the Lord, for. he shall send Jesus Christ, who before was preached unto you." The time of redemption here had reference to the time when Christ should come; then, and not till then, would their sins be blotted out. Why? Because they were murderers, and no murderer hath eternal life. Even David must wait for those times of refreshing, before he can come forth and his sins be blotted out. For Peter, speaking of him says, "David hath not yet ascended into heaven, for his sepulcher is with us to this day." His remains were then in the tomb.' Now, we read that many bodies of the saints arose at Christ's resurrection, probably all the saints, but it seems that David did not. Why? Because he had been a murderer. If the ministers of religion had a proper understanding of the doctrine of eternal judgment, they would not be found attending the man who forfeited his life to the injured laws of his country, by shedding innocent blood; for such characters cannot be forgiven until they have paid the last farthing. The prayers of all the ministers in the

world can never close the gates of hell against a murderer. (Joseph
Smith, DPJS, 341)

OBEDIENCE

THE NECESSITY FOR OBEDIENCE TO GOD'S COMMANDMENTS

To get salvation we must not only do some things, but everything which God has commanded. Men may preach and practice
everything except those things which God commands us to do, and
will be damned at last. We may tithe mint and rue, and all manner
of herbs, and still not obey the commandments of God. The object
with me is to obey and teach others to obey God in just what he
tells us to do. It mattereth not whether the principle is popular or
unpopular, I will always maintain a true principle, even if I stand
alone in it. (Joseph Smith, HC 6:223.)

OBEDIENCE MUST BE VOLUNTARY

Obedience is a requirement of heaven and is therefore a principle
of the gospel. Are all required to be obedient? Yes, all. 'What, against
their will? Oh, no, not by any means. There is no power given to
man, nor means lawful to be used to compel men to obey the will of
God against their wish, except persuasion and good advice, but there
is a penalty attached to disobedience, which all must suffer who will
not obey the obvious truths or laws of heaven. (Joseph F. Smith, JD 19:193.)

MEN ARE JUDGED ON OBEDIENCE

God judges men according to the use they make of the light
which he gives them. (Joseph Smith, DPJS, 343)

HOW LONG MUST WE KEEP GOD'S COMMANDMENTS

"If ye love me, keep my commandments .... "

How long? For a day? Keep the commandments of the Lord for
a week? Observe and do his will for a month or a year? There is
no promise to any individual, that I have any knowledge of, that he
shall receive the reward of the just, unless he is faithful to the end.
If we fully understand and faithfully carry out in our lives the saying of Jesus, "If ye love me, keep my commandments," we shall
be prepared to go back and dwell in the presence of the Father and
the Son ....

All God's requirements tend to do good to his children. Any notion to the contrary is the result of ignorance. (Brigham Young, JD 13:310-311.)

SALVATION DEPENDS ON OBEDIENCE

I realize that the salvation of this people does not depend upon the great amount of teaching, instruction, or revelation that is given unto them, but their salvation depends more upon their obeying the commandments of God which are given unto them, their becoming a doer of the word, and following the counsel of those who are set to lead them. (Wilford Woodruff, JD 4: 190.)

TEST GOSPEL PRINCIPLES THROUGH OBEDIENCE

Evidences are not enough to gain a testimony of the truth; we have something more. I was brought up in scientific laboratories, where I was taught to test things, never to be satisfied unless a thing was tested. We have the right to test the gospel of the Lord Jesus Christ. By testing it I mean living it, trying it out. Do you question the Word of Wisdom? Try it. Do you question the law of tithing? Practice it. Do you doubt the virtue of attending meetings? Attend them. Only then shall we be able to speak of these things intelligently and in such a way as to be respected by those who listen to us. Those who live the gospel of Jesus Christ gain this higher knowledge, this greater testimony, this ultimate assurance that this is the truth. It is the way to truth. All the while, we must seek help from the great unseen world about us, from God and his messengers. We call that prayer. A man never finds perfect peace, never reaches afar unless he penetrates to some degree the unseen world, and reaches out to touch the hands, as it were, of those who live in that unseen world, the world out of which we came, the world into which we shall go. (John A. Widtsoe, CR October 1938, 129.)

OPPOSITION

WHAT CAN YOU KNOW EXCEPT BY OPPOSITES

What can you know, except by its opposite? Who could number the days, if there were no nights to divide the day from the night? Angels could not enjoy the blessings of light eternal, were there no darkness. All that are exalted and all that will be exalted will be exalted upon this principle. If I do not taste the pangs of death in my mortal body, I never shall know the enjoyment of eternal life. If I do not know pain, I cannot enjoy ease. If I am not acquainted with the dark, the gloomy, the sorrowful, I cannot enjoy the light, the joyous, the felicitous that are ordained for man. No person, either in heaven or upon earth, can enjoy and understand these things upon any other principle. (Brigham Young, JD 8:28.)

NECESSARY THAT TWO POWERS EXIST

I find in tracing out the scriptures, that from the beginning there have existed two powers-the powers of light and the powers of darkness; that both these things existed in the heavens before they came here, that the powers of darkness were cast out, and thus became the devil and his angels. This antagonism, then, existed before, and it is necessary it should exist. It is necessary men should be tried and purged and purified and made perfect through suffering. (John Taylor, JD 20:305.)

OPPOSITION IN ALL THINGS

Can the people comprehend that there is not, has not been, and never can be any method, scheme, or plan devised by any being in. this world for intelligence to eternally exist and obtain an exaltation, without knowing the good and the evil-without tasting the bitter and the sweet. Can the people understand that it is actually necessary for opposite principles to be placed before them, or this state of being would be no probation and we should have no opportunity for exercising the agency given us? Can they understand that we cannot obtain eternal life unless we actually know and comprehend by our experience the principle of good and the principle of evil, the light and the darkness, truth, virtue, and holiness-also vice, wickedness, and corruption? (Brigham Young, JD 7:237.)

THE OPPOSITES WERE PERMITTED ON EARTH

Darkness and sin were permitted to come on this earth. Man partook of the forbidden fruit in accordance with a plan devised from eternity, that mankind might be brought in contact with the principles and powers of darkness, that they might know the bitter and the sweet, the good and the evil, and be able to discern between light and darkness, to enable them to receive light continually. (Brigham Young, JD 7:158.)

TWO SPIRITS STRIVING WITH MEN ALWAYS

There are two spirits striving with all men-one telling them what to do that is right, and one telling them what to do that will please themselves, that will gratify their own pride and ambition. If we live as we ought to live, we will always follow that spirit that teaches us to do that which is right. (Heber J. Grant, CR April 1938, 12.)

THERE MUST NEEDS BE AN OPPOSITION

Sin is in the world, but it is not necessary that we should sin, because sin is in the world; but, to the contrary, it is necessary that we should resist sin, and for this purpose is sin necessary. Sin exists in all the eternities. Sin is co-eternal with righteousness, for it must needs be that there is an opposition in all things. (Brigham Young, JD 10:2-3.)

PEACE

PEACE COMES BY CONFORMING TO THE GOSPEL

Though we are living in perilous times, you and I can rejoice because the gospel is among men. The Church is established in this free country, never more to be thrown down or given to another people. Nations may rise, and nations may destroy each other in strife, but this gospel is here to stay, and we must preach it and proclaim it, that peace may come, for it is only through obedience to the gospel of Jesus Christ that peace will come permanently upon the earth. (David O. McKay, DNCS January 2, 1952, 4.)

THE KEY TO PEACE IS THE GOSPEL

There is only one thing that can bring peace into the world. It is the adoption of the gospel of Jesus Christ, rightly understood, obeyed and practiced by rulers and people alike....'It is being preached in power to all nations, kindreds, tongues and peoples of the world, by the Latter-day Saints, and the day is not far distant when its message of salvation shall sink deep into the hearts of the common people, who, in sincerity and earnestness, when the time comes, will not only surely register their judgment against a false Christianity, but against war and the makers of war as crimes against the human race. For years it has been held that peace comes only by preparation for war; the present conflict should prove that peace comes only by preparing for peace, through training the people in righteousness and justice, and seeking rulers who respect the righteous will of the people.

Not long hence and the voice of the people shall be obeyed, and the true gospel of peace shall dominate the hearts of the mighty. It will then be impossible for war lords to have power over the life and death of millions of men:as they now have, to decree the ruin of commerce, industry, and Vowing fields, or to cause untold mental agony and human misery like plague and pestilence to prevail over the nations. It looks much as if, after the devastation of wars, as promised in the scriptures,... the self-constituted monarchs must give way to rulers chosen by the people, who shall be guided by the doctrines of love and peace as taught in the gospel of our Lord. There will then be instituted a new social order in which the welfare of all shall be uppermost, and all shall be permitted to live in the utmost liberty and happiness. (Joseph F. Smith, IE 17:1074.)

THE PEACE OF CHRIST

Jesus Christ says, "my peace I give unto you: not as the world giveth, give I unto you." (John 14:27.) Wherever this peace exists, it leaves an influence that is comforting and refreshing to the souls of those who partake of it. It is like the morning dew to the thirsty plant. This peace is the gift of God alone, and it can be received only from him through obedience to his laws. If any man wishes to introduce peace into his family or among his friends, let him cultivate it in his own bosom; for sterling peace can only be had according to the legitimate rule and authority of heaven, and obedience to its laws. (John Taylor, JD 1:228.)

PEACE COMES BY OBEDIENCE TO LAW

The peace of Christ does not come by seeking the superficial things of life, neither does it come except as it springs from the individual's heart. Jesus said to his disciples: "Peace I leave with you. My peace I give unto you; not as the world giveth, give I unto you." Thus the Son of man as the executor of his own will and testament gave to his disciples and to mankind the "first of all human blessings." It was a bequest conditioned upon obedience to the principles of the Gospel of Jesus Christ. It is thus bequeathed to each individual. No man is at peace with himself or his God who is untrue to his better self, who transgresses the law of right either in dealing with himself by indulging in passion, in appetite, yielding to temptations against his accusing conscience, or in dealing with his fellowmen, being untrue to their trust. Peace does not come to the transgressor of law; peace comes by obedience to law, and it is that message which Jesus would have us proclaim among men. (David O. McKay, CR October 1938, 133.)

PERFECTION

ATTAINING PERFECTION

Begin at a small point; can you not live to the Lord for one minute? Yes. Then can we not multiply that by sixty and make an hour, and live that hour to the Lord? Yes; and then for a day, a week, a month, and a year? Then, when the year is past, it has been spent most satisfactorily. (Brigham Young, JD 8:59-60.)

PERFECTION CAN BE LIVED

Can mortal beings live so that they are worthy of the society of angels? I can answer the question for myself–I believe that they can; I am sure that they can. But in doing this, they must subdue the sin that is within themselves, correct every influence that arises within their own hearts that is opposed to the sanctifying influences of the grace of God, and purify themselves by their faith and by their conduct, so that they are worthy. Then they are prepared for the society of angels. To be saints indeed requires every wrong influence that is within them, as individuals, to be subdued, until every evil desire is eradicated, and every feeling of their hearts is brought into subjection to the will of Christ. (Brigham Young, JD 19:66-67.)

PERFECTION IN THIS LIFE

I do not expect that any of us will ever become in mortality quite so perfect as God is perfect; but in the spheres in which we are called to act, and according to the capacity and breadth of intelligence that we possess, in our sphere, and in the existence of the talent, the ability, and intelligence that God has given to us, we may become as perfect in our sphere as God is perfect in his higher and more exalted sphere. I believe that. (Joseph F. Smith, CR April 1915, 140.)

THE TERM "PERFECTION" APPLIED

When we use the term perfection, it applies to man in his present condition, as well as to heavenly beings. We are now, or may be, as perfect in our sphere as God and angels are in theirs, but the greatest intelligence in existence can continually ascend to greater heights of perfection. (Brigham Young, JD 1:93.)

GO ON TO PERFECTION

We are none of us entirely perfect; but we expect to "go on unto perfection," by keeping the will and word of the Lord. By and by we will arrive at that position when we will receive our bodies, quickened with the power of an endless life, and they become spiritual; and our spirits, which are the sons and the daughters of God, are embodied in them to be continued-to be continued, to be unrestricted in their united existence; not for a time or a season; spirit and element inseparably connected, receiving a fullness of joy. And the time will come when we will receive that grand glory, a resurrection of our mortal bodies to become spiritually united with our spiritual beings, the sons and the daughters of God, and all eternity will be before us and will open to us glory and honor and power and dominion and increase, perpetually, forever and ever. That is what is coming to us, and it will pay us for all the difficulties and troubles through which we are called upon to pass sometimes, here in this mortal state. (Charles W. Penrose, CR October 1923, 18.)

PHILOSOPHY

THE PLAN OF SALVATION IS NATURAL PHILOSOPHY

What do you know on natural principles? I do not say natural philosophy, because my religion is natural philosophy. You never heard me preach a doctrine but what has a natural system to it, and, when understood, is as easy to comprehend as that two and two equal four. All the revelations of the Lord Almighty to the children of men, and all revealed doctrines of salvation are upon natural principles, upon natural philosophy. When I use this term, I use it as synonymous with the plan of salvation; natural philosophy is the plan of salvation, and the plan of salvation is natural philosophy. (Brigham Young, JD 4:202-203.)

FACT, THEORY, AND INFERENCE AMONG PHILOSOPHERS

We have a great many ignorant, learned fools. But when you

meet sensible, intelligent men... they will acknowledge principle when it is presented to them. But many men have not the understanding to do it. Talking about saving themselves, who among the philosophers can save themselves?... What do they do when they have to grapple with the sting of death, and when it stares them in the face? Why, they take a leap in the dark. And this darkness is the end of all their philosophy and all their science. And the little they do know in divining the laws of God is only with regard to some very few of the fundamental principles of those laws that God has planted everywhere throughout the universe, and I do not therefore have that reverence for their theories, notions, and vagaries, nor do I attach that importance to their intelligence that some people do ....

If we have to submit to their theories, we should really be in a sorry condition. (John Taylor, JD 20:119-120.)

PHILOSOPHIC THEORIES NO SUBSTITUTE FOR THE GOSPEL

Philosophic theories of life have their place and use, but it is not in the classes of the Church schools, and particularly are they out of place here or anywhere else, when they seek to supplant the revelations of God. The ordinary student cannot delve into these subjects deep enough to make them of any practical use to him, and a smattering of knowledge in this line only tends to upset his simple faith in the gospel, which is of more value to him in life than all the learning of the world without it.

The religion of the Latter-day Saints is not hostile to any truth, nor to scientific search for truth. "That which is demonstrated, we accept with joy," said the First Presidency in their Christmas greeting to the saints, "but vain philosophy, human theory and mere speculations of men we do not accept, nor do we adopt anything contrary to divine revelation or to good common sense, but everything that tends to right conduct, that harmonizes with sound morality and increases faith in Deity, finds favor with us, no matter where it may be found."

A good motto for young people to adopt, who are determined to delve into philosophic theories, is to search all things, but be careful to hold on only to that which is true. The truth persists, but the theories of philosophers change and are overthrown. What men use today as a scaffolding for scientific purposes from which to reach out into the unknown for truth, may be torn down tomorrow, having served its purpose; but faith is an eternal principle through which the humble believer may secure everlasting solace. It is the only way to find God.

Science and philosophy through all the ages have undergone change after change. Scarcely a century has passed but they have introduced new theories of science and philosophy, that supersede the old traditions and the old faith and the old doctrines entertained by philosophers and scientists. These things may undergo continuous changes, but the word of God is always true, is always right. The principles of the gospel are always true, the principles of faith in God, repentance from sin, baptism for the remission of sins by authority of God, and the laying on of hands for the gift of the Holy Ghost-these principles are always true, and are always absolutely necessary for the salvation of the children of men, no matter who they are and where they are. No other name under heaven is given but that of Jesus Christ, by which you can be saved or exalted in the kingdom of God. Not only has God declared them, not only has Christ declared these principles, by his voice to his disciples, from generation to generation, in the old time, but in these latter days, they have taken up the same testimony and declared these things to the world. They are true today as they were then, and we must obey these things. (Joseph F. Smith, IE 14:548.)

PRAYER

FAMILY PRAYER BEFORE OTHER THINGS
When you get up in the morning, before you suffer yourselves to eat one mouthful of food, call your wife and children together, bow down before the Lord, ask him to forgive your sins, and protect you through the day, to preserve you from temptation and all evil, to guide your steps aright, that you may do something that day that shall be beneficial to the kingdom of God on the earth. Have you time to do this? Elders, sisters, have you time to pray? (Brigham Young, JD 15:36.)

PRAYER FOR WORLD
Now, in conclusion, may I offer a humble prayer in behalf of the Church and the nation and the world. I realize that there is

much more that might bc said, but in this prayer may I indulge and ask that you might unite your faith with mine for a few moments:

"Our heavenly and eternal Father, hear our prayer this day, and sanctify it to our good all that is being done by righteous men and women in the Church and throughout the world to bring to naught the evils that are rolling over the world like an avalanche. Increase within us the zeal to bring thy great plan of redemption to every nation, kindred, tongue, and people, looking to that glorious day when thy prophecy will be realized when truth will cover the earth as waters cover the mighty deep.

"We appeal to the protection of thy almighty power to that end which accords with thy purpose concerning us and thy work. We put ourselves under the surveillance of thy watchful eye and pray that thou will never leave us alone, and continue to give the guidance necessary to the accomplishment of thy purposes."

I add to that humble prayer my witness to the members of this church and to the world that through the atonement of the Lord Jesus Christ, "all mankind may be saved by obedience to the laws and ordinances of the Gospel." (Article of Faith 3.)

This is indeed the Lord's work in which we are engaged. lie lives and is ever ready to draw near to us when we prepare ourselves to be worthy to draw close to him. From my own personal experience, I know this, which I declare in all soberness to be true, and in the name of the Lord Jesus Christ. Amen. (Harold B. Lee, CR, Oct. 1972, 64).

PRAYERS SHOULD BE ORIGINAL

It is not good for us to pray by rote, to kneel down and repeat the Lord's prayer continually. I think that one of the greatest follies I have ever witnessed is the foolish custom of men repeating the Lord's prayer continually without considering its meaning....It thus becomes only a form; there is no power in it; neither is it acceptable, because it is not offered from the heart, nor with the understanding; and I think that it is desirable for us to look well to our words when we call upon the Lord .... Let us speak the simple words, expressing our need, that will appeal most truly to the Giver of every good and perfect gift. He can hear us in secret; and he knows the desires of our hearts before we ask, but he has made it obligatory and a duty that we shall call upon his name. (Joseph F. Smith, IE 11:730-731 .)

HAVE FAITH IN PRAYER

I have more faith in prayer before the Lord than almost any other principle on earth. If we have no faith in prayer to God, we have not much in either him or the gospel. We should pray unto the Lord, asking him for what we want. Let the prayers of this people ascend before the Lord continually in the season thereof, and the Lord will not turn them away, but they will be heard and answered, and the kingdom and Zion of God will rise and shine, she will put on her beautiful garments and be clothed with the glory of her God and fulfill the object of her organization here upon the earth. (Wilford Woodruff, JD 17:249.)

PRAY FOR FELLOWSHIP OF THE HOLY GHOST

I was inducted into the kingdom of God by prayer, and I have been sustained by the Almighty Father by prayer ever since that day. I do not pray for form's sake. I pray because I earnestly desire to have the fellowship of the Holy Ghost. I cannot understand how anybody can pray for form's sake, although I have almost been led to believe that we do so on a great many times and occasions, and I will give you my reasons for so thinking. What is the idea, after singing, of one of the brethren standing up here to open this meeting by prayer? Is he not our spokesman, the mouthpiece, and should we not, while he utters the sentences, have those sentences pass through our minds in a prayer as a congregation, and when he has finished it, endorse the same by saying "amen." What is the meaning of amen? So be it. Well, I noticed today that there were few   "amens." Why is this? Did we not endorse the prayer? Did we not sanction it? I should think if we did we would naturally say "amen"-so let it be ....What is the meaning of prayer? Why, it is to earnestly ask something that we require with all our hearts. All who are in fellowship of the Holy Ghost, will ask God for his Spirit to be in their hearts in all their business relations even, that they might not soil their hands, but keep them clean and their hearts pure, and that they might merit his approbation. The Lord Jesus Christ encouraged his disciples to pray-to pray without ceasing. (George Teasdale, JD 26:50-51.)

ADVICE TO THE BRETHREN ON PRAYER

We would say to the brethren, seek to know God in your closets, call upon him in the fields. Follow the directions of the Book of Mormon, and pray over, and for your families, your cattle, your flocks, your herds, your corn, and all things that you possess; ask the blessing of God upon all your labors, and everything that you engage in. Be virtuous and pure; be men of integrity and truth; keep the commandments of God; and then you will be able more perfectly to understand the difference between right and wrong-between the things of God and the things of men; and your path will be like that of the just, which shineth brighter and brighter unto the perfect day. (Joseph Smith, DPJS, 213.)

PRAY IN FAITH FOR OUR NEEDS
I fear, as a people, we do not pray enough, in faith. We should call upon the Lord in mighty prayer and make all our wants known unto him. For if he does not protect and deliver us and save us, no other power will. Therefore our trust is entirely in him. Therefore our prayers should ascend into the ears of our Heavenly Father day and night. (Wilford Woodruff, MS 48:806.)

PRE-EXISTENCE

THE SPIRIT OF MAN NOT CREATED
The spirit of man is not a created being; it existed from eternity, and will exist to eternity. Anything created cannot be eternal; and earth, water, etc., had their existence in an elementary state, from eternity. Our Savior speaks of children and says, their angels always stand before my Father. The Father called all spirits before him at the creation of man, and organized them. He [Adam] is the head, and was told to multiply. The keys were first given to him, and by him to others. He will have to give an account of his stewardship, and they to him. (Joseph Smith, DPJS, 125.)

WE DWELT WITH THE FATHER AND THE SON
With regard to our position before we came here, I will say that we dwelt with the Father and with the Son, as expressed in the hymn, "O My Father." ... We dwelt in the presence of God before we came here. (Wilford Woodruff, MS 56:229.)

WE WERE PRESENT IN THE COUNCIL IN HEAVEN
Where did we come from? From God. Our spirits existed before they came to this world. They were in the councils of the heavens

before the foundations of the earth were laid. We were there. We sang together with the heavenly hosts for joy when the foundations of the earth were laid and when the plan of our existence upon this earth and redemption were mapped out we were there; we were interested and we took part in this great preparation. We were unquestionably present in those councils when that wonderful circumstance occurred... when Satan offered himself as a savior of the world if he could but receive the honor and glory of the Father for doing it .... We were, no doubt, there and took part in all those scenes, we were vitally concerned in the carrying out of these great plans and purposes, we understood them, and it was for our sakes they were decreed and are to be consummated. (Joseph F. Smith, JD 25:57.)

WE ARE THE OFFSPRING OF OUR FATHER IN HEAVEN

We believe that we are the offspring of our Father in heaven, and that we possess in our spiritual organizations the same capabilities, powers and faculties that our Father possesses, although in an infantile state, requiring to pass through a certain course or ordeal by which they will be developed and improved according to the heed we give to the principles we have received .... We are born in the image of God our Father; he begot us like unto himself. There is the nature of Deity in the composition of our spiritual organization; in our spiritual birth our Father transmitted to us the capabilities, powers and faculties which he himself possessed, as much so as the child on its mother's bosom possesses, although in an undeveloped state, the faculties, powers and susceptibilities of its parent. (Lorenzo Snow, JD 14:300, 302.)

WE ARE ACQUAINTED WITH OUR HEAVENLY PARENTS

I want to tell you, each and every one of you, that you are well acquainted with God our Heavenly Father, or the great Elohim. You are all well acquainted with him, for there is not a soul of you but what has lived in his house and dwelt with him year after year; and yet you are seeking to become acquainted with him, when the fact is, you have merely forgotten what you did know ....

There is not a person here today but what is a son or a daughter of that Being. In the spirit world their spirits were first begotten and brought forth, and they lived there with their parents for ages before they came here. This, perhaps, is hard for many to believe, but it is the greatest nonsense in the world not to believe it. If you do not believe it, cease to call him Father; and when you pray, pray to some other character. (Brigham Young, JD 4:216.)

WE SAW THE SAVIOR CHOSEN IN HEAVEN

The first step in the salvation of man is the law of eternal and self-existent principles. Spirits are eternal. At the first organization in heaven we were all present, and saw the Savior chosen and appointed, and the plan of salvation made, and we sanctioned it. (Joseph Smith, CDG 288.)

WE MADE THE DECISION TO COME TO EARTH

I dare say that in the spirit world, when it was proposed to us to come into this probation and pass through the experience that we are now receiving, it was not altogether pleasant and agreeable; the prospects were not so delightful in all respects as might have been desired. Yet there is no doubt that we saw and understood clearly there, that, in order to accomplish our exaltation and glory, this was a necessary experience; and however disagreeable it might have appeared to us, we were willing to conform to the will of God, and consequently we are here. (Lorenzo Snow, MS 56:49.)

PRIESTHOOD

PRIESTHOOD HAS EXISTED WITH GOD FROM ETERNITY

The priesthood is an everlasting principle, and existed with God from eternity, and will to eternity, without beginning of days or end of years. The keys have to be brought from heaven whenever the gospel is sent. When they are revealed from heaven, it is by Adam's authority ....

The priesthood is everlasting. The Savior, Moses, and Elias, gave the keys to Peter, James, and John, on the mount, when they were transfigured before him. The priesthood is everlasting-without beginning of days or end of years; without father, mother, etc. If there is no change of ordinances, there is no change of priesthood Wherever the ordinances of the gospel are administered, there is the priesthood.

How have we come by the priesthood in the last days? It came down, down in regular succession. Peter, James and John had it given to them and they gave it to others. Christ is the great high priest; Adam next. (Joseph Smith, DPJS, 48.)

PRIESTHOOD IS GOVERNING LAW

The priesthood of the Son of God... is the law by which the worlds are, were, and will continue for ever and ever. It is that system which brings worlds into existence and peoples them, gives them their revolutions-their days, weeks, months, years, their seasons and times and by which they ... go into a higher state of existence- (Brigham Young, JD 15:127.)

PRIESTHOOD IS THE ONLY LEGITIMATE POWER

It [the priesthood] is the rule and government of God, whether on earth or in the heaven; and it is the only legitimate power, the only authority that is acknowledged by him to rule and regulate the affairs of his kingdom. When every wrong thing shall be put right and all usurpers shall be put down, when he whose right it is to reign shall take the dominion, then nothing but the priesthood will bear rule; it alone will sway the scepter of authority in heaven and on earth, for this is the legitimacy of God. (John Taylor, JD 1:224.)

RESPONSIBILITY OF THE PRIESTHOOD

As we study the various activities like family home evening and the activities pertaining to temple marriage, home teaching, and what not, we have discovered that we never make any headway by mere exhortation and trying to pressure people into holding home evenings or home teaching. We are discovering that the only way to get home teaching over, or to get family home evening going, or attendance at sacrament meeting, or to have more temple marriages or temple attendance, is to make sure that the holder of the priesthood in the home magnifies his priesthood: and until he can realize the importance of the priesthood of God, which gives him the power of Almighty God to act through him, that home is not going to be secure.

We must impress upon every father that he will be held responsible for the eternal welfare of his family: that means coming into the Church with his family; that means going to sacrament meeting with his family; that means holding family home evenings to keep his family intact; it means preparing himself to take them to the temple, so that there can be prepared thereby the steps that will make for an eternal family home.

It is a high responsibility to impress upon priesthood holders how they magnify their priesthood by living and doing as the Lord has commanded. (Harold B. Lee, CR, April 1972, 117)

PRIESTHOOD CAN ONLY BE USED RIGHTEOUSLY

If we as apostles, bearing the Holy Priesthood, use that priesthood for any other purpose under heaven but to build up the kingdom of God, if we do our power will fall like lightning from heaven. A good many men have undertaken this-men high in the Priesthood, even the apostleship-to build themselves up upon the ' authority of the priesthood. And where have they gone? You may amen to their power and authority. They have lost their bishopric and apostleship. Let us reflect on these things. I say the same to myself. I say the same to the apostles, seventies, and high priests. You cannot use the priesthood for any other purpose under heaven but to build up the kingdom and do the will of God; and when you attempt to do otherwise your power will be taken from you. (Wilford Woodruff, CR April 1880, 83.)

TITLES OF THE PRIESTHOOD ARE SACRED

The titles "prophet, seer and revelator," "apostles," etc.....are too sacred to be used indiscriminately in our common talk. There are occasions when they are quite proper and in place; but in our everyday conversations it is sufficient honor to address any brother holding the Melchizedek Priesthood as eider. The term elder is a general one, applying to all those who hold the higher priesthood, whether they be apostles, patriarchs, high priests or seventies; and to address a brother as Apostle So-and-So, or Patriarch Such-a-One in the common talk of business and the like is using titles too sacred to be in place on such occasion ....The use of all these titles continuously and indiscriminately savors somewhat of blasphemy and is not pleasing to our Heavenly Father. (Joseph F. Smith, JI 38:20.)

DISTINCTION BETWEEN KEYS OF THE PRIESTHOOD AND PRIESTHOOD

The priesthood in general is the authority given to man to act for God. Every man ordained to any degree of the priesthood, has this authority delegated to him.

But it is necessary that every act performed under this authority shall be done at the proper time and place, in the proper way, and after the proper order. The power of directing these labors constitutes the keys of the priesthood. In their fullness, the keys are held by only one person at a time, the prophet and president of the Church. He may delegate any portion of this power to another, in which case that person holds the keys of that particular labor. Thus, the president of a temple, the president of a stake, the bishop of a ward, the president of a mission, the president of a quorum, each holds the keys of the labors performed in that particular body or locality. His priesthood is not increased by this special appointment, for a seventy who presides over a mission has no more priesthood than a seventy who labors under his direction; and the president of an elders' quorum, for example, has no more priesthood than any member of that quorum. But he holds the power of directing the official labors performed in the mission or the quorum, or in other words, the keys of that division of that work. So it is throughout all the ramifications of the priesthood-a distinction must be carefully made between the general authority, and the directing of the labors performed by that authority. (Joseph F. Smith, IE 4:230.)

JOSEPH SMITH LIVED UNTIL HE RECEIVED EVERY KEY, ORDINANCE, AND LAW

He [Joseph Smith] lived until he received every key, ordinance and law ever given to any man on the earth, from Father Adam down, touching this dispensation. He received powers and keys from under the hands of Moses for gathering the house of Israel in the last days; he received under the hands of Elijah the keys of sealing the hearts of the fathers to the children and the hearts of the children to the fathers; he received under the hands of Peter, James and John, the apostleship, and everything belonging thereto; he received under the hands of Moroni all the keys and powers required of the stick of Joseph in the hands of Ephraim; he received under the hands of John the Baptist the Aaronic Priesthood, with all its keys and powers, and every other key and power belonging to this dispensation, and I am not ashamed to say that he was a prophet of God, and he laid the foundation of the greatest work and dispensation that has ever been established on the earth. (Wilford Woodruff, JD 16:267.)

THE PRIESTHOOD GREATER THAN ANY OF ITS OFFICES

There is no office growing out of this priesthood that is or can be greater than the priesthood itself. It is from the priesthood that the office derives its authority and power. No office gives authority to the priesthood. No office adds to the power of the priesthood. If our brethren would get this principle thoroughly established in their minds, there would be less misunderstanding in relation to the functions of government in the Church than there is. Today the question is, which is the greater-the high priest or the seventy, the seventy or the high priest? I tell you that neither of them is the greater, and neither of them is the lesser. Their callings lie in different directions, but they are from the same priesthood. If it were necessary, the seventy, holding the Melchizedek Priesthood, as he does, I say if it were necessary, he could ordain a high priest; and if it were necessary for a high priest to ordain a seventy, he could do that. Why? Because both of them hold the Melchizedek Priesthood. Then again, if it were necessary, though I do not expect the necessity will ever arise, and there was no man left on earth holding the Melchizedek Priesthood, except an elder-that elder, by the inspiration of the Spirit of God and by the direction of the Almighty, could proceed, and should proceed, to organize the Church of Jesus Christ in all its perfection, because he holds the Melchizedek Priesthood. But the house of God is a house of order, and while the other officers remain in the Church, we must observe the order of the priesthood, and we must perform ordinances and ordinations strictly in accordance with that order, as it has been established in the Church through the instrumentality of the Prophet Joseph Smith and his successors. (Joseph F. Smith, CR October 1903, 87.)

HOW TO OBTAIN A FULLNESS OF THE PRIESTHOOD OF GOD

If a man gets a fullness of the priesthood of God, he has to get it in the same way that Jesus Christ obtained it, and that was by keeping all the commandments and obeying all the ordinances of the house of the Lord. (Joseph Smith, DPJS, 51.)

THE PROPHET UNLOCKED THE PRISON DOORS

Why did he [the Lord] call him [Joseph Smith] unto the spirit world? Because he held the keys of this dispensation, not only before he came to this world and while he was in the flesh, but he would hold them throughout the endless ages of eternity. He held the keys of past generations-of the millions of people who dwelt on the earth in the fifty generations that had passed and gone who had not the law of the gospel, who never saw a prophet, never saw an apostle, never heard the voice of any man who was inspired of God and had power to teach them the gospel of Christ, and to organize the church of Christ on earth. He went to unlock the prison doors of these people, as far as they would receive his testimony, and the saints of God who dwell in the flesh wilt build temples and perform certain ordinances for the redemption of the dead. This was the work of Joseph the Prophet in the spirit world. (Wilford Woodruff, CR April 1880,8.)

THE POWER OF THE PRIESTHOOD EXTENDS BEYOND THE GRAVE

When... any man holding the priesthood officiates, he administers by the authority of the Lord Jesus 'Christ; then that priesthood has effect, and all the blessings that a servant of God bestows upon the children of men will take effect both in this life and in that which is to come. If I have a blessing given to me by the Holy Priesthood, or if I receive a blessing from a patriarch, those gifts and blessings will reach into the other world; and if I am true to my covenants through this life, I can claim every blessing that has been conferred upon me, because that authority by which they were conferred is ordained of God; and it is that authority by which the sons of the Most High administer unto the children of men the ordinances of life and salvation; and those official acts will have their effect upon those persons beyond the grave as well as in this life. (Wilford Woodruff, JD 9:162-163.)

PROPHETS, SEERS, AND REVELATORS

PROPHETS DIRECTED BY REVELATION

The Lord never had-and never will have to the end of time-a Church on the earth without prophets, apostles, and inspired men. Whenever the Lord had a people on the earth that he acknowledged as such, that people were led by revelation. (Wilford Woodruff, JD 24:240.)

PROPHECY WILL BE FULFILLED

You need have no fear that when one of the apostles of the Lord Jesus Christ delivers a prophecy in the name of Jesus Christ, because he is inspired to do that, that it will fall by the wayside. I know of more than one prophecy, which, looking at it naturally, seemed as though it would fall to the ground as year after year passed. But lo and behold, in the providences of the Lord, that prophecy was fulfilled. (Heber J. Grant, IE 40:735.)

PROPHETS, SEERS, AND REVELATORS

"Can a number of men be prophets, seers, and revelators, and yet not interfere with the fights of him who stands at the head?"...

On March 27, 1836, the Prophet Joseph Smith called upon the "quorums and congregation of saints to acknowledge the Twelve Apostles who were present as prophets, seers and revelators," and they were thus sustained. Their being ordained to this authority and sustained as such does not lead to confusion nor to the least conflict of authority, any more than the reception of the gift of prophecy by the elders leads to any conflict between them and the President of the Church. (George Q. Cannon, JI 26:27-28.)

PRE-EMINENCE OF THE PRESIDENT OF THE CHURCH

Joseph Smith was given two counselors, the three forming the First Presidency of the Church. (March 18, 1833.) This was preceded in March 8, 1833, by a revelation declaring that "Through you [Joseph Smith] shall the oracles be given to another, even unto the Church." The preeminence of the President of the Church was maintained. The question as to whether the counselors held the same power as the President was soon debated among the people. What could the counselors do without direct appointment from the President? These questions were answered in a meeting on January 26, 1836. The Prophet there said, "The Twelve are not subject to any other than the First Presidency... and where I am not, there is no First Presidency over the Twelve." In other words, were the President taken, the counselors would have no authority. The counselors do not possess the power of the President and cannot act in Church matters without direction and consent of the President.

All this defined clearly the position and authority of the President of the Church. (John A. Widtsoe, JS 303.)

THE TESTIMONY OF JESUS IS THE SPIRIT OF PROPHECY

If any person should ask me if I were a prophet, I should not deny it, as that would give me the lie; for, according to John, the testimony of Jesus is the spirit of prophecy; therefore, if I profess to be a witness or teacher and have not the spirit of prophecy, which is the testimony of Jesus, I must be a false witness; but if I be a true teacher and witness, I must possess the spirit of prophecy, and that constitutes a prophet; and any man who says he is a teacher or preacher of righteousness and denies the spirit of prophecy is a liar, and the truth is not in him; and by this key false teachers and impostors may be detected. (Joseph Smith, DPJS, 178)

GOD DETERMINES WHO SHALL STAND AT THE HEAD

You need have no fear, my dear brothers and sisters, that any man will ever stand at the head of the Church of Jesus Christ unless our Heavenly Father wants him to be there. (Heber J. Grant, IE 40:735.)

HOW THE PRESIDENT OF THE CHURCH IS DETERMINED

Do you know of any reason in case of the death of the President of the Church why the Twelve Apostles should not choose some other than the President of the Twelve to be the President of the Church?

I know of several reasons why they should not. First, at the death of the President of the Church the Twelve Apostles become the presiding authority of the Church, and the president of the Twelve is really the President of the Church, by virtue of his office as much while presiding over the Twelve Apostles as while presiding over his two counselors .... Second, in case of the death of the President of the Church, it takes a majority of the Twelve Apostles to appoint the President of the Church, and it is very unreasonable to suppose that the majority of that quorum could be converted to depart from the course marked out by inspiration and followed by the apostles at the death of Christ and by the Twelve Apostles at the death of Joseph Smith. (Wilford Woodruff, WW 561.)

THE OFFICE OF PRESIDENT OF THE CHURCH

I have the right to bless. I hold the keys of the Melchizedek

Priesthood and of the office and power of patriarch. It is my right to bless; for all the keys and authority and power pertaining to the government of the Church and to the Melchizedek and Aaronic Priesthood are centered in the presiding officers of the Church. There is no business, nor office, within the Church that the President of the Church may not fill, and may not do, if it is necessary, or if it is required of him to do it. He holds the office of patriarch; he holds the office Of high priest and of apostle, of seventy, of elder, of bishop, and of priest, teacher and deacon in the Church; all these belong to the Presidency of The Church of Jesus Christ of Latter-day Saints, and they can officiate in any and in all of these callings when occasion requires. (Joseph F. Smith, CR October 1915, 7.)

PROPHECY FULFILLED

A few years ago, we had a woman who had written some scurrilous things about the Prophet Joseph Smith. (Mention was made of it here in the conference at that time.) Shortly thereafter, I met someone on the street and they asked me if there had been a revelation or an utterance at the recently concluded general conference that might be considered as a prophecy. And I said, "Did you hear the closing remarks of President George Albert Smith as he closed the conference? If you did, you heard a prophet speaking, and let me tell you what he said." I happened to have a clipping in my wallet. This is what President George Albert Smith said:

"Many have belittled Joseph Smith, but those who have will be forgotten in the remains of mother earth, and the odor of their infamy will ever be with them, but honor, majesty, and fidelity to God, exemplified by Joseph Smith and attached to his name, will never die."

No truer words were ever spoken.... (Harold B. Lee, CR, Oct. 1973, 166.)

REPENTANCE

REPENTANCE-A RESOLVE TO SIN NO MORE

Repentance is not that superficial sorrow felt by the wrongdoer when "caught in the act"-a sorrow not for sin, but for sin's detection. Chagrin is not repentance. Mortification and shame alone bring no change of heart toward right feeling and right living.

Even remorse is not all there is to repentance. In highest meaning and fullest measure, repentance is equivalent to reformation; the beginning of the reformatory process being a resolve to "sin no more."" .... by this ye may know that a man repenteth of his sins: Behold he will confess them and forsake them." (Orson F. Whitney, SNT, 239.)

DAILY REPENTANCE NOT VALID

Repentance is a thing that cannot be trifled with every day. Daily transgression and daily repentance is not that which is pleasing in the sight of God. (Joseph Smith, DPJS, 85.)

DEATHBED REPENTANCE NOT ACCEPTABLE

We should take warning and not wait for the deathbed to repent, as we see the infant taken away by death, so may the youth and middle-aged as well as the infant be suddenly called into eternity. Let this, then, prove as a warning to all not to procrastinate repentance, or wait till a deathbed, for it is the will of God that man should repent and serve him in health, and in the strength and power of his mind in order to secure his blessing, and not wait until he is called to die. (Joseph Smith, HC 4:554.)

WHOEVER SINS MUST REPENT

God is no respecter of persons. He who sins in this Church, be it a small or a great transgression, must repent. It matters not in whom the sin may be found. In the President of the Church? Yes. In his counselors? Yes. In the Twelve Apostles? Yes. The presidents of the stakes, the bishops of wards, and the leaders of Zion? Yes. In the lay members of the Church? Yes. It affects the most influential as well as the humblest in the Church. When children come to years of understanding and accountability, must they repent and forsake sin? Yes. (Rudger Clawson, CR October 1904, 36.)

COME BACK AND CARRY ON

I invite all members of the Church to live with ever more attention to the life and example of the Lord Jesus Christ, especially the love and hope and compassion He displayed.

"I pray that we might treat each other with more kindness, more courtesy, more humility and patience and forgiveness. We do have high expectations of one another, and all can improve. Our world cries out for more disciplined living of the commandments of God. But the way we are to encourage that, as the Lord told the Prophet Joseph in the wintry depths of Liberty Jail, is 'by persuasion, by long-suffering, by gentleness and meekness, and by love unfeigned;...without hypocrisy, and without guile' (D&C 121:41-42).

"To those who have transgressed or been offended, we say, come back. To those who are hurt and struggling and afraid, we say, let us stand with you and dry your tears. To those who are confused and assailed by error on every side, we say, come to the God of all truth and the Church of continuing revelation. Come back. Stand with us. Carry on. Be believing. All is well, and all will be well. Feast at the table laid before you in The Church of Jesus Christ of Latter-day Saints and,Strive to follow the Good Shepherd who has provided it. Have hope, exert faith, receive-and give charity, the pure love of Christ. (Howard W. Hunter, ES, July, 1994, 4-5.)

GIVE AWAY ALL OUR SINS

Contrition is costly—it costs us our pride and our insensitivity, but it especially costs us our sins. For, as King Lamoni's father knew twenty centuries ago, this is the price o!true hope. "O God," he cried, "wilt thou make thyself known unto me, and I will give away all my sins to know thee... that I may be raised from the dead, and be saved at the last day." (Alma 22:18.) When we, too, are willing to give away all our sins to know him and follow him, we, too, will be filled with the joy of eternal life. (Howard W. Hunter, ES, May 1993, 64.)

TRUE REPENTANCE INVOLVES FORSAKING OUR SINS

True repentance is not only sorrow for sins and humble penitence and contrition before God, but it involves the necessity of turning away from them, a discontinuance of all evil practices and deeds, a thorough reformation of life, a vital change from evil to good, from vice to virtue, from darkness to light. Not only so, but to make restitution, so far as it is possible, for all the wrongs we have done, to pay our debts, and restore to God and man their rights-that which is due them from us. This is true repentance, and the exercise of the will and all the powers of body and mind is demanded to complete this glorious work of repentance; then God will accept it. (Joseph F. Smith, JD 19:190.)

RESURRECTION

A VISION OF THE RESURRECTION

Would you think it strange if I relate what I have seen in vision in relation to this interesting theme? Those who have died in Jesus Christ may expect to enter into all that fruition of joy when they come forth, which they possessed or anticipated here.

So plain was the vision. that I actually saw men, before they had ascended from the tomb, as though they were getting up slowly. They took each other, "My father, my son, my mother, my daughter, my brother, my sister." And when the voice calls for the dead to arise, suppose I am laid by the side of my father, what would be the first joy of my heart? To meet my father, my mother, my brother, my sister; and when they are by my side, I embrace them and they me. (Joseph Smith, DPJS, 158.)

WE RISE AS WE DIED

They must rise just as they died; we can there hail our lovely infants with the same glory-the same loveliness in the celestial glory, where they all enjoy alike. They differ in stature, in size, the same glorious spirit gives them the likeness of glory and bloom; the old man with his silvery hairs will glory in bloom and beauty. No man can describe it to you-no man can write it. (Joseph Smith, DPJS, 156.)

CHILDREN WILL GROW AFTER THE RESURRECTION

Little children who are taken away in infancy and innocence before they have reached the years of accountability and are capable of committing sin, the gospel reveals to us the fact that they are redeemed, and Satan has not power over them; neither has death any power over them. They are redeemed by the blood of Christ, and they are saved just as surely as death has come into the world through the fall of our first parents .... Joseph Smith declared that the mother who laid down her little child, being deprived of the privilege, the joy, and the satisfaction of bringing it up to manhood or womanhood in this world, would, after the resurrection, have all the joy, satisfaction and pleasure, and even more than it would have been possible to have had in mortality, in seeing her child grow to the full measure of the stature of its spirit. (Joseph F. Smith, MS 57:388-389.)

THE FUNDAMENTAL PARTS, OF ONE'S BODY NEVER BECOME A PART OF ANOTHER'S BODY

There is no fundamental principle belonging to a human system that ever goes into another in this world or in the world to come; I care not what the theories of men are. We have the testimony that God will raise us up, and he has the power to do it. If anyone supposes that any part of our bodies, that is, the fundamental parts thereof, ever goes into another body, he is mistaken. (Joseph Smith, DPJS, 159.)

RESURRECTION, A TRUE PRINCIPLE

I know that some people of very limited comprehension will say that all the parts of the body cannot be brought together, for, say they, the fish probably have eaten them up, or the whole may have been blown to the four winds of heaven. It is true the body, or the organization, may be destroyed in various ways, but it is not true that the particles out of which it was created can be destroyed. They are eternal; they never were created. This is not only a principle associated with our religion, or in other words, with the great science of life, but also it is in accordance with acknowledged science. You may take, for instance, a handful of fine gold, and scatter it in the street among the dust; again, gather together the materials among which you have thrown the gold, and you can separate one from the other so thoroughly, that your handful of gold can be returned to you; yes, every grain of it. You may take particles of silver, iron, copper, lead, and mix them together with any other ingredients, and there are certain principles connected with them by which these different materials can be eliminated, every particle cleaving to that of its own element. (John Taylor, JD 18:333-334.)

FLESH IS QUICKENED BY THE SPIRIT

When our flesh is quickened by the Spirit, there will be no blood in this tabernacle. (Joseph Smith, HC 6:366.)

BLOOD HAS NO PART IN THE RESURRECTION

The blood he spilled upon Mount Calvary he did not receive again into his veins. That was poured out, and when he was resurrected, another element took the place of the blood. It will be so with every person who receives a resurrection; the blood will not be resurrected with the body, being designed only to sustain the life of the present organization. When that is dissolved, and we again obtain our bodies by the power of the resurrection, that which we now call the life of the body, and which is formed from the food we eat and the water we drink will be supplanted by another element; for flesh and blood cannot inherit the kingdom of God. (Brigham Young, JD 7:163.)

ALL LOSSES WILL BE MADE UP IN THE RESURRECTION

All your losses will be made up to you in the resurrection, provided you continue faithful. By the vision of the Almighty I have seen it. (Joseph Smith, DPJS, 159.)

CHRIST'S RESURRECTION

We believe that Christ... was crucified upon the cross, that he died, his spirit leaving his body, and was buried and was on the third day resurrected, his spirit and body re-uniting,... That he is a resurrected being, and that in his pattern every man, woman, and child that ever lived shall come forth from the grave a resurrected being, even as Christ is a resurrected being. (Heber J. Grant, MS 99:395-396.)

NO DISEASE IN RESURRECTION.

If a man has gone through life with a club foot, or other deformity, will he be raised in the resurrection and have the club foot or deformity, and have to wait until the "restoration of all things," before this imperfection is corrected?

The answer to this is, No! Let us carry this a little farther. If a person through disease passes through the greater part of his life with some deformity—such as diabetes, tumors, consumption—will he have to be subject to such disease until the day of "restitution of all things?" Certainly not, and it is just as inconsistent to claim that the club foot would have to remain as to say that any of these other deformities or diseases would have to remain.

CHILDREN RESURRECTED AS CHILDREN

Of course, children who die do not grow in the grave. They will come forth with their bodies as they were laid down, and then they will grow to the full stature of manhood or womanhood after the resurrection, but all will have their bodies fully restored. (Joseph Fielding Smith, D.S., II, 293.)

VISION OF THE RESURRECTION GIVEN TO WILFORD WOODRUFF

After laboring in that part of Memphis, Tennessee, for a length of time, I received a letter from Joseph Smith and Oliver Cowdery, in which they requested me to stay in that country and take charge of the churches that we had built up there. The Prophet promised me many things, and said I should lose no blessings by tarrying in that country and doing as he wished me, and letting the other brethren go and get their endowments. I was then at the house of Brother Abraham O. Smoot's mother. I received this about sundown. I went into a little room where there was a sofa, to pray alone. I felt full of joy and rejoicing at the promises God had made to me through the Prophet. While I was upon my knees praying, my room was filled with light. I looked and a messenger stood by my side. I arose, and this personage told me he had come to instruct me. He presented before me a panorama. He told me he wanted me to see with my eyes and understand with my mind what was coming to pass in the earth before the coming of the Son of Man. He commenced with what the revelations say about the sun being turned to darkness, the moon to blood, and the stars falling from heaven. Those things were all presented to me one after another, as they will be, I suppose, when they are manifest before the coming of the Son of Man. Then he showed me the resurrection of the dead-what is termed the first and second resurrection. In the first resurrection I saw no graves nor anyone raised from the grave. I saw legions of celestial beings, men and women who had received the gospel all clothed in white robes. In the form they were presented to me, they had already been raised from the grave. After this he showed me what is termed the second resurrection. Vast fields of graves were before me, and the Spirit of God rested upon the earth like a shower of gentle rain, and when that fell upon the graves they were opened, and an immense host of human beings came forth.' They were just as diversified in their dress as we are here, or as they were laid down. This personage taught me with regard to these things. (Wilford Woodruff, MS 76:612.)

THE BEAUTY OF A RESURRECTED PERSON

Nothing is so beautiful as a person in a resurrected and glorified condition. There is nothing more lovely than to be in this condition and have our wives and children and friends with us. (Lorenzo Snow, CR October 1900, 63.)

REVELATION

NO ERROR IN THE REVELATIONS

I [Joseph Smith] never told you I was perfect; but there is no error in the revelations which I have taught. (Joseph Smith, DPJS, 66.)

REVELATION IS A PRIVILEGE OF THE PRIESTHOOD

One great privilege of the priesthood is to obtain revelations of the mind and will of God. (Joseph Smith, DPJS, 68.)

THE HOLY GHOST A REVELATOR

No man can receive the Holy Ghost without receiving revelations. The Holy Ghost is a revelator. (Joseph Smith, DPJS, 65.)

THE SPIRIT OF REVELATION

A person may profit by noticing the first intimation of the spirit of revelation; for instance, when you feel pure intelligence flowing into you, it may give you sudden strokes of ideas, so that by noticing it you may find it fulfilled the same day or soon; (i.e.,) those things that were presented unto your minds by the Spirit of God will come to pass; and thus by learning the Spirit of God and understanding it you may grow into the principle of revelation, until you become perfect in Christ Jesus. (Joseph Smith, DPJS, 65-66.)

SPECIAL REVELATION AND HOW OBTAINED

We never inquire at the hand of God for special revelation only in case of there being no previous revelation to suit the case; and that in a council of high priests ....

It is a great thing to inquire at the hands of God or to come into his presence; and we feel fearful to approach him on subjects that are of little or no consequence to satisfy the queries of individuals, especially about things the knowledge of which men ought to obtain, in all sincerity, before God, for themselves, in humility by the prayer of faith; and more especially a teacher or a high priest in the Church. (Joseph Smith, DPJS, 66.)

HOW REVELATION IS RECEIVED

All things whatsoever God in his infinite wisdom has seen fit and proper to reveal to us, while we are dwelling in mortality, in regard to our mortal bodies, are revealed to us in the abstract, and independent of affinity of this mortal tabernacle, but are revealed to our spirits precisely as though we had no bodies at all; and those revelations which will save our spirits will save our bodies. God reveals them to us in view of no eternal dissolution of the body, or tabernacle. (Joseph Smith, DPJS, 65.)

REVELATION NEEDED FOR TIME AND CIRCUM-STANCE

We require a living tree-a living fountain-living intelligence, proceeding from the living priesthood in heaven, through the living priesthood on earth .... And from the time that Adam first received a communication from God, to the time that John, on the Isle of Patmos, received his communication, or Joseph Smith had the heavens opened to him, it always required new revelations, adapted to the peculiar circumstances in which the churches or individuals were placed. Adam's revelation did not instruct Noah to build his ark; nor did Noah's revelation tell Lot to forsake Sodom; nor did either of these speak of the departure of the children of Israel from Egypt. These all had revelations for themselves, and so had Isaiah, Jeremiah, Ezekiel, Jesus, Peter, Paul, John, and Joseph. And so must we, or we shall make a shipwreck. (John Taylor, MS 9:323-324.)

REVELATION NOT TO BE RECEIVED FOR ONE OF HIGHER AUTHORITY

I will inform you that it is contrary to the economy of God for any member of the Church, or anyone, to receive instruction for those in authority, higher than themselves; therefore you will see the impropriety of giving heed to them; but if any person have a vision or a visitation from a heavenly messenger, it must be for his own benefit and instruction; for the fundamental principles, government, and doctrine of the Church are vested in the keys of the kingdom. (Joseph Smith, DPJS, 66.)

EVERY GREAT OR GOOD THING COMES FROM GOD

If there was anything great or good in the world, it came from God. The construction of the first vessel was given to Noah, by revelation. The design of the ark was given by God, "a pattern of heavenly things." The learning of the Egyptians, and their knowledge of astronomy was no doubt taught them by Abraham and

Joseph, as their records testify, who received it from the Lord. The art of working in brass, silver, gold, and precious stones, was taught by revelation, in the wilderness. The architectural designs of the Temple at Jerusalem, together with its ornaments and beauty, were given of God. Wisdom to govern the house of Israel was given to Solomon, and to the judges of Israel; and if he had always been their king, and they subject to his mandate, and obedient to his laws, they would still have been a great and mighty people-the rulers of the universe, and the wonder of the world.

If Nebuchadnezzar, or Darius, or Cyrus, or any other king possessed knowledge or power, it was from the same source, as the scriptures abundantly testify. (Joseph Smith, DPJS, 201-202.)

MEN SHOULD BELIEVE IN THE REVELATIONS OF GOD

I [Joseph Smith] believe all that God ever revealed, and I never hear of a man being damned for believing too much; but they are damned for unbelief. (Joseph Smith, DPJS, 67.)

SATAN HAS GREAT POWER

It is not every revelation that is of God, for Satan has the power to transform himself into an angel of light; he can give visions and revelations as well as spiritual manifestations and table-rappings. (John Taylor, MS 19: 197.)

NO MAN BY HIS OWN SEARCHING CAN FIND OUT GOD

No man by his own researches can find out God. He may, by reason and reflection, by observing and pondering upon the wonders of creation, by studying his own internal and external nature, come to the sure conclusion that there is a God, and to a very small extent make an estimate of his character. But without the Almighty manifests himself in some manner, finite man can never obtain a knowledge of infinite Deity. The speculations of human beings concerning God are many and various, and a vast number of their conclusions inconsistent and vain. Human learning, no matter how extensive, and human research, no matter how profound, are of necessity inadequate alone to the acquisition of a knowledge of divine things. Hence an unlettered person enlightened direct from God, will know more of Deity than the most erudite collegian who has not received this divine illumination. (Charles W. Penrose, Mormon Doctrine, 11 .)

SABBATH DAY

THE SABBATH IS FOR WORSHIP
Sunday is worship day. It is holy. This is a Christian nation, and the Lord has promised that as long as we keep him in mind and worship him this country will stand-this Government will stand. No other nation can take it or destroy it. But if we forget him, God's promises are not binding.

Why should Sunday be observed as a day of rest? First, Sunday is essential to the true development and strength of body, and that is a principle which we should proclaim more generally abroad, and practice ....

A second purpose for keeping holy the Sabbath day is: "That thou mayest more fully keep thyself unspotted from the world." Contemplation during that sacred hour, self-communion, and higher than that, communion in thoughts and feeling with the Lord-the realization that he is near enough to be aware of what you are thinking ....

Keep thyself unspotted from the world, and ask God to forgive you if you have in mind injuring anyone who trusts you-I mean morally-or if you have in mind wronging anybody, cleanse it from your mind. Read Doctrine and Covenants section 59.

A third purpose for keeping holy the Sabbath day is a law of God, resounding through the ages from Mount Sinai. You cannot transgress the law of God without circumscribing your spirit. Finally, our Sabbath, the first day of the week, commemorates the greatest event in all history: Christ's resurrection and his visit as a resurrected being to his assembled apostles. His birth, or course, was necessary, and just as great, so I say this is one of the greatest events in all history. (David O. McKay, CR October 1956, 90-91.)

THE IMPORTANCE OF SABBATH DAY OBSERVANCE
I feel that it is a reproach to the Latter-day Saints that we should have amusements in our towns and cities on the day of the Lord. As the years come and go, and young men and young women go to their ruin because of losing their respect for the Sabbath and the sacredness of the day, I feel that the men who have sat in the legis-

lature, and who have failed to protect us against the evil, will have much to answer for. (Heber J. Grant, IE 39:660.)

BREAKING SABBATH CONTRARY TO LAW OF GOD

I am opposed to Sabbath-breaking. It is wrong. It is contrary to the law of God. It is a transgression of the commandment of the Lord. I am opposed to men, women and children going to pleasure resorts on the Sabbath day. (Joseph F. Smith, MS 56:710.)

THE NEED FOR A SUNDAY LAW

I am decidedly and emphatically in favor of a Sunday law which will not only prevent the playing of baseball but will also provide for the closing of theatres and other places of amusement. (Heber J. Grant, IE 16:262-263.)

THE RESULTS OF BREAKING THE SABBATH

This very day upon which we meet here to worship, viz., the Sabbath, has become the play-day of this great nation-the day set apart by thousands to violate the commandment that God gave long, long ago, and I am persuaded that much of the sorrow and distress that is afflicting and will continue to inflict mankind is traceable to the fact that they have ignored his admonition to keep the Sabbath day holy. (George Albert Smith, CR October 1935, 120.)

SACRAMENT

WE SHOULD NOT PARTAKE OF THE SACRAMENT UNWORTHILY

Previous to the administration, I spoke of the propriety of this institution in the Church, and urged the importance of doing it with acceptance before the Lord, and asked: How long do you suppose a man may partake of this ordinance [the sacrament] unworthily, and the Lord not withdraw his Spirit from him? How long will he thus trifle with sacred things, and the Lord not give him over to the buffetings of Satan until the day of redemption?... Therefore our hearts ought to be humble, and we to repent of our sins, and put away evil from among us. (Joseph Smith, DPJS, 215.)

THREE THINGS TO REMEMBER WHEN TAKING THE SACRAMENT

"It is expedient that the Church meet together often." We meet in the house of God not as mere acquaintances suspicious of one another, but as brethren in the brotherhood of Christ. We meet in the presence of him who has said, "Love one another .... "

Do we always stop to think, on that sacred Sabbath day when we meet together to partake of the sacrament, that we witness, promise, obligate ourselves, in the presence of God, that we will do certain things? Note them. I have time merely to mention them.

The first: That we are willing to take upon ourselves the name of the Son. In so doing we choose him as our leader and our ideal; and he is the one perfect character in all the world. It is a glorious thing to be a member of the Church of Christ and to be called a Christian in the true sense of the term; and we promise that we should like to be that, that we are willing to do it.

Secondly, that we will always remember him. Not just on Sunday, but on Monday, in our daily acts, in our self-control. When our brother hurts us are we going to try to master our feelings and not retaliate in the same spirit of anger? When a brother treats us with contempt, are we going to try to return kindness? That's the spirit of the Christ and that's what we are promised,–that we will do our best to achieve these high standards of Christianity, true Christian principles.

The third: We promise to "keep the commandments which he has given." Tithing, fast offerings, the Word of Wisdom, kindness, forgiveness, love. The obligation of a member of the Church of Christ is great, but it is as glorious as it is great, because obedience to these principles gives life eternal. On the other hand, the man who seeks to live by violating the principles is deceived by the adversary and goes the way to death. (David O. McKay, CR October 1929, 10-11, 14.)

IMPORTANCE OF THE SACRAMENT OF THE LORD'S SUPPER

We have met to partake of the sacrament of the Lord's Supper, and we should endeavor to draw away our feelings and affections from things of time and sense. For in partaking of the sacrament we not only commemorate the death and sufferings of our Lord and Savior Jesus Christ, but we also shadow forth the time when he will come again and when we shall meet and eat bread with him in the kingdom of God. When we are thus assembled together, we may expect to receive guidance and blessings from God. (John Taylor, JD 14:185.)

THE SACRAMENT MEETING SHOULD PROMOTE UNITY

My observation has taught me, and I believe all will agree, that no person can regularly go to the meetings of the Church and mingle with his brethren and sisters without catching the spirit of the work and developing within him a warmth of affection and a fervor of devotion which will tend to make him one with his fellows. The sacrament meeting which was given of the Lord by revelation is designed specifically to promote unity. We are even admonished not to partake of the sacrament if we entertain unkindly feelings in our hearts toward others. (Stephen L Richards, CR October 1938, 117.)

SALVATION

THE GREAT PLAN OF SALVATION

The great plan of salvation is a theme which ought to occupy our strict attention, and be regarded as one of heaven's best gifts to mankind. No consideration whatever ought to deter us from showing ourselves approved in the sight of God, according to his divine requirement. Men not infrequently forget that they are dependent upon heaven for every blessing which they are permitted to enjoy, and that for every opportunity granted them they are to give an account. You know, brethren, that when the Master in the Savior's parable of the stewards called his servants before him he gave them several talents to improve on while he should tarry abroad for a little season, and when he returned, he called for an accounting. So it is now. Our Master is absent only for a little season, and at the end of it he will call each to render an account; and where the five talents were bestowed, ten will be required; and he that has made no improvement will be cast out as an unprofitable servant, while the faithful will enjoy everlasting honors. Therefore we earnestly implore the grace of our Father to rest upon you, through Jesus Christ his Son, that you may not faint in the hour of temptation, nor be overcome in the time of persecution. (Joseph Smith, DPJS, 81-82.)

SALVATION COMES THROUGH GOSPEL ORDINANCES

No man ever did or ever will obtain salvation only through the ordinances of the gospel and through the name of Jesus. There can be no change in the gospel; all men that are saved from Adam to infinitum are saved by the one system of salvation. The Lord may give many laws and many commandments to suit the varied circumstances and conditions of his children throughout the world, such as giving a law of carnal commandment to Israel, but the laws and principles of the gospel do not change. (Wilford Woodruff, JD 10:217.)

JESUS HAS PROVIDED SALVATION FOR MANKIND

Now, the inquiry on our minds is, are all the world going to share in these blessings? Yes, all the world. Are there none going to be lost? Are there none going to suffer the wrath of the Almighty? I can say, in the first place, as I have said all my life, where I have been preaching, I never had the spirit to preach hell and damnation to the people. I have tried a great many times-I tried last Sabbath, and I have tried today to come to that point-the sufferings of the wicked. They will suffer, it seems; but I cannot get my heart upon anything else, only salvation for the people. All nations are going to share in these blessings; all are incorporated in the redemption of the Savior. He has tasted death for every man; they are all in his power, and he saves them all, as he says, except the sons of perdition; and the Father has put all the creations upon this earth in his power. The earth itself, and mankind upon it, the brute beasts, the fish of the sea, and the fowls of heaven, the insects, and every creeping thing with all things pertaining to this earthly ball-all are in the hands of the Savior, and he has redeemed them all. (Brigham Young, JD 6:296-297.)

SALVATION-A PLAN AS WIDE AS ETERNITY

We talk sometimes about cooperation; but the plan of salvation, if you please, is a grand cooperative scheme, as expansive as the heavens and as wide as eternity; it penetrates through all time, extends through all ages, and reaches men in every position, living or dead; they who have lived, we who now live, and they who will live hereafter are all working together in this grand cooperative plan, and we cannot be made perfect without our progenitors, neither can they be perfected without us, and they are as much dependent upon us as we are dependent upon them. We can build temples, they cannot; it is not their province to administer in them at present, but it is ours, and we are called upon to do so. They are interested in our welfare, they are our fathers, we are their children; they are laboring there, we here, for our mutual salvation and exaltation in the kingdom of God....The living and the dead so-called in Christ are all working for the accomplishment of the same great objects and purposes. Don't you think that they, behind the veil, feel as much interested in the work as we do? Read the little glimpse given by John in Revelation, where he speaks about the souls of those before the altar; who prayed day and night that he would avenge them of their adversaries and again, when the time came when Babylon was cast down there was rejoicing among the angels in heaven. This gives us some faint idea of the feelings entertained by those on the other side of the veil in relation to events here. (John Taylor, JD 17:374.)

SCRIPTURES

SEARCH THE SCRIPTURES

Search the scriptures-search the revelations which we publish and ask your Heavenly Father, in the name of his Son Jesus Christ, to manifest the truth unto you, and if you do it with an eye single to his glory, nothing doubting, he will answer you by the power of his Holy Spirit. You will then know for yourselves and not for another. (Joseph Smith, HC 1:282.)

THE SCRIPTURES WILL REMAIN

The Bible, the Book of Mormon, the book of Doctrine and Covenants contain the words of eternal life unto this generation, and they will rise in judgment against those who reject them. (Wilford Woodruff, JD 22:335.)

THE SCRIPTURES-THE BETTER PART OF THIS WORLD'S LITERATURE

The Bible, Book of Mormon, Doctrine and Covenants, and Pearl of Great Price do not contain the wisdom of men alone, but of God. While they do not find their way into the homes of many people, they contain the word of the Lord. What mattereth it though we understand Homer and Shakespeare and Milton, and I might enumerate all the great writers of the world, if we have failed to read the scriptures we have missed the better part of this world's literature. (George Albert Smith, CR October 1917, 43.)

THE SCRIPTURES LIKENED TO A LIGHTHOUSE

The Old and New Testaments, the Book of Mormon, and the book of Doctrine and Covenants... are like a lighthouse in the ocean or a fingerpost which points out the road we should travel. Where do they point? To the fountain of light....That is what these books are for. They are of God; they are invaluable and necessary; by them we can establish the doctrine of Christ. (Brigham Young, JD 8:129.)

SCRIPTURE

"I find that when I get casual in my relationships with divinity and when it seems that no divine ear is listening and no divine voice is speaking, that I am far, far away. If I immerse myself in the scriptures the distance narrows and the spirituality returns. I find myself loving more intensely those whom I must love with all my heart and mind and strength, and loving them more, I find it easier to abide their counsel." (Spencer W. Kimball, Address to Seminary and Institute Teachers, BYU, 11 July1966.)

SEEK TO UNDERSTAND THE SCRIPTURES AS THEY ARE

The people on every hand are inquiring, "What does this scripture mean, and how shall we understand this or that passage?" Now I wish, my brethren and sisters for us to understand things precisely as they are, and not as the flitting, changing imagination of the human mind may frame them.

The Bible is just as plain and easy of comprehension as the revelation which I have just read to you [Doctrine and Covenants, 18], if you understand the Spirit of God the spirit of revelation and know how the gospel of salvation is adapted to the capacity of weak man. (Brigham Young, JD 3:336.)

SECOND COMING OF CHRIST

THE SECOND COMING OF CHRIST AND EVENTS PRECEDING IT

The coming of the Son of Man never will be-never can be till the judgments spoken of for this hour are poured out; which judgments are commenced. Paul says, "Ye are the children of the light, and not of the darkness, that that day should overtake you as a thief in the night." It is not the design of the Almighty to come upon the earth and crush it and grind it to powder, but he will reveal it to his servants and prophets.

Judah must return, Jerusalem must be rebuilt, and the temple, and water come out from under the temple, and the waters of the Dead Sea be healed. It will take some time to rebuild the walls of the city and the temple, etc.; and all this must be done before the Son of Man will make his appearance. There will be wars and rumors of wars, signs in the heavens above and on the earth beneath, the sun turned into darkness and the moon to blood, earthquakes in divers places, the seas heaving beyond their bounds; then will appear one grand sign of the Son of Man in heaven. But what will the world do? They will say it is a planet, a comet, etc. But the Son of Man will come as the sign of the coming of the Son of Man, which will be as the light of the morning cometh out of the east. (Joseph Smith, DPJS, 236-237.)

SIGNS OF THE SECOND COMING HAVE COMMENCED

I will prophesy that the signs of the coming of the Son of Man are already commenced. One pestilence will desolate after another. We shall soon have war and bloodshed. The moon will be turned into blood. I testify of these things and that the coming of the Son of Man is nigh, even at your doors. (Joseph Smith, HC 3:390.)

THE TIME OF THE SECOND COMING OF CHRIST NOT REVEALED

Jesus Christ never did reveal to any man the precise time that he would come. Go and read the scriptures, and you cannot find anything that specifies the exact hour he would come; and all that say so are false teachers. (Joseph Smith, DPJS, 230.)

THE SECOND COMING OF CHRIST NOT A GREAT DISTANCE AWAY

You and I live in a day in which the Lord our God has set his hand for the last time, to gather out the righteous and to prepare a people to reign on this earth,-a people who will be purified by good works, who will abide the faith of the living God and be ready to meet the Bridegroom when he comes to reign over the earth, even Jesus Christ... and be prepared for that glorious event-the coming of the Son of Man-which I believe will not be at any great distant day. (Joseph F. Smith, MS 36:220.)

GOSPEL TO BE PREACHED IN ALL THE WORLD BEFORE THE SECOND COMING OF CHRIST

A sure indication of the great event [second coming of Christ], as specified by the Lord himself, was and is that the gospel of the kingdom shall be preached in all the world. The missionary service of The Church of Jesus Christ of Latter-day Saints attests the progressive fulfillment of this prediction. (Heber J. Grant, MS 91:34.)

JEWS TO RETURN BEFORE THE SECOND COMING OF CHRIST

He will never come until the Jews are gathered home and have rebuilt their temple and city and the Gentiles have gone up there to battle against them. He will never come until his Saints have built up Zion and have fulfilled the revelations which have been spoken concerning it. He will never come until the Gentiles throughout the whole Christian world have been warned by the inspired elders of Israel. (Wilford Woodruff, JD 18:111.)

THE JEWS AND THE SECOND COMING

We have a great desire for their welfare, and are looking for the time soon to come when they will gather to Jerusalem, build up the city and the land of Palestine, and prepare for the coming of the Messiah. When he comes again, he will not come as he did when the Jews rejected him; neither will he appear first at Jerusalem when he makes his second appearance on the earth; but he will appear first on the land where he commenced his work in the beginning, and planted the Garden of Eden, and that was done in the land of America.

When the Savior visits Jerusalem, and the Jews look upon him, and see the wounds in his hands and in his side and in his feet, they will then know that they have persecuted and put to death the true Messiah, and then they will acknowledge him, but not till then. They have confounded his first and second coming, expecting his first coming to be as a mighty prince instead of as a servant. They will go back by and by to Jerusalem and own their

Lord and Master. We have no feelings against them. (Brigham Young, JD 11: 279.)

THE SECOND COMING OF CHRIST WILL NOT BE DELAYED

The Lord Jesus Christ is coming to reign on earth. The world may say that he delays his coming until the end of the earth. But they know neither the thoughts nor the ways of the Lord. The Lord will not delay his coming because of their unbelief, and the signs both in heaven and earth indicate that it is near. The fig trees are leafing in sight of all the nations of the earth, and if they had the Spirit of God they could see and understand them. (Wilford Woodruff, JD 16:35.)

IT IS THE ELEVENTH HOUR

Do you know that it is the eleventh hour of the reign of Satan on the earth? Jesus is coming to reign, and all you who fear and tremble because of your enemies, cease to fear them and learn to fear to offend God, fear to transgress his laws, fear to do any evil to your brother, or to any being upon the earth, and do not fear Satan and his power, nor those who have only power to slay the body, for God will preserve his people. (Brigham Young, JD 10:250.)

SELF-CONTROL

THE POWER OF THOUGHT

What a man continually thinks about determines his actions in times of opportunity and stress. A man's reaction to his appetites and impulses when they are aroused gives the measure of that man's character. In these reactions are revealed the man's power to govern or his forced servility to yield. (David O. McKay, CR October 1951,8.)

MAN MUST BE MASTER OF HIMSELF

No man is safe unless he is master of himself; and there is no tyrant more merciless or more to be dreaded than an uncontrollable appetite or passion. We will find that if we give way to the groveling appetites of the flesh and follow them up, that the end will be invariably bitter, injurious and sorrowful, both to the individual and society. It is hurtful in example as well as in its individual effects; dangerous and hurtful to the unwary; while the

denial of these appetites-the crucifixion of the flesh, so to speak-
and an aspiration for something noble; whenever possible, doing
good to our fellow creatures, hoping for the future, laying up trea-
sures in heaven, where moth and rust cannot corrupt, and where
thieves cannot break through and steal-all these things will bring
everlasting happiness; happiness for this world and the world to
come. If there is no pleasure in the world except that which we
experience in the gratification of our physical desires-eating,
drinking, gay associations, and the pleasures of the world-then the
enjoyments of the world are bubbles, there is nothing in them,
there is no lasting benefit or happiness to be derived from them.
(Joseph F. Smith, DW 33:130.)

SELF-MASTERY

I commend to you, young man and young woman, the virtue of
self-mastery, if you would fulfill the true measure of your life in
subduing, in order to realize the ideal, the spiritual development of
your soul. (David O. McKay, DNCS September 6, 1952, 15.)

IMPORTANCE OF CONTROLLING OUR THOUGHTS

As a child, thirteen years of age, I went to school at the
Brigham Young Academy. It was fortunate that part of my instruction came under Dr. Karl G. Maeser, that outstanding educator
who was the first builder of our Church schools. I cannot remember much of what was said during the year that I was there, but
there is one thing that I will probably never forget. I have repeated
it many times; I think I have told it in this building. Dr. Maeser
one day stood up and said:

"Not only will you be held accountable for the things you do,
but you will be held responsible for the very thoughts you think."

Being a boy, not in the habit of controlling my thoughts very
much, it was quite a puzzle to me what I was to do, and it worried
me. In fact, it stuck to me just like a burr. About a week or ten
days after that it suddenly came to me what he meant. I could see
the philosophy of it then. All at once there came to me this interpretation of what he had said: Why, of course you will be held
accountable for your thoughts, because when your life is completed in mortality, it will be the sum of your thoughts. That one sug-
gestion has been a great blessing to me all my life, and it has
enabled me upon many occasions to avoid thinking improperly,

because I realize that I will be, when my life's labor is complete, the product of my thoughts. (George Albert Smith, DNCS February 16, 1946.)

WE MUST LEARN TO GOVERN OUR ACTIONS

We have a great mission to perform-we have to try to govern ourselves according to the laws of the kingdom of God, and we find it one of the most difficult tasks we ever undertook, to learn to govern ourselves, our appetites, our dispositions, our habits, our feelings, our lives, our spirits, our judgment, and to bring all our desires into subjection to the law of the kingdom of God and to the spirit of truth. (John Taylor, JD 9:12.)

SELF-CONTROL SHOULD BEGIN IN CHILDHOOD

The lesson of self-control should begin in childhood, in the' home. Little children should have a sense of freedom to do as they wish up to a certain point. Beyond that point they cannot go, and that is when that freedom interferes with the rights, comfort or convenience of another member of the family.

I have told before about an incident that occurred in a zoo. It is simple, and some probably may think we should not go to the monkeys for lessons. I think they can teach us some. Sister McKay and I stood one day, I believe it was at San Diego, watching a mother monkey with a new born babe. She was guarding it, her quick eye watching the other monkeys in the cage; but the little babe was free to do just as it pleased, hopping around, weak in its infancy, getting hold of the bars, starting to climb. When it would reach a certain place, the mother would reach up and bring it back. When it got into a danger point, that mother instinctively guarded it and said, "Back this way." And then the babe was free again, but only within certain limits.

I said to Sister McKay, "There is a lesson of life in guiding children." (David O. McKay, CR September 1950, 165.)

SPIRITS AND SPIRIT CHILDREN

GOD IS THE FATHER OF OUR SPIRITS

It does seem strange that so many people doubt our divine ancestry, and that God is the Father of our spirits; yet from the very beginning, from the very earliest period of which we have any record in this world, he has been teaching men and women this fact...

When God created the earth and placed our first parents upon
. it, he did not leave them without knowledge concerning himself. It is true that there had been taken from them the remembrance of their pre-existent life, but in his tender mercy he talked
with them and later he sent his choice servants to instruct them in
the things pertaining to eternal life. (George Albert Smith, CR October
1922, 90-91.)

ALL SPIRITS ARE COMPOSED OF SUBSTANCE

In tracing the thing to the foundation, and looking at it philo-
sophically, we shall find a very material difference between the
body and the spirit; the body is supposed to be organized matter,
and the spirit, by man is thought to be immaterial, without substance. With this latter statement we should beg leave to differ,
and state that spirit is a substance; that it is material, but that it is
more pure, elastic and refined matter than the body; that it existed
before the body, can exist in the body; and will exist separate
from the body, when the body will be mouldering in the dust; and
will in the resurrection be again united with it. (Joseph Smith, HC
4:575.)

THE SPIRITS OF MEN ARE ETERNAL

I would just remark, that the spirits of men are eternal, that they
are governed by the same priesthood that Abraham, Melchizedek,
and the Apostles were: that they are organized according to that
priesthood which is everlasting, "without beginning of days or end
of years"-that they all move in their respective spheres, and are
governed by the law of God; that when they appear upon the earth
they are in a probationary state, and are preparing, if righteous, for
a future and greater glory; that the spirits of good men cannot
interfere with the wicked beyond their prescribed bounds, for
Michael, the Archangel, dared not bring a railing accusation
against the devil, but said, "The Lord rebuke thee, Satan." (Joseph
Smith, HC 4:575-576)

CERTAIN SPIRITS HAVE TO BE BORN INTO THIS WORLD

The spirits which are reserved have to be born into the world,
and the Lord will prepare some way for them to have tabernacles.
(Brigham Young, JD 3:264.)

THE SPIRIT IS PURE

You are aware that many think that the devil has rule and power over both body and spirit. Now, I want to tell you that he does not hold any power over man, only so far as the body overcomes the spirit that is in a man, through yielding to the spirit of evil. The spirit that the Lord puts into tabernacle of flesh is under the dictation of the Lord Almighty, but the spirit and body are united in order that the spirit may have a tabernacle, and be exalted; and the spirit is influenced by the body and the body by the spirit.

In the first place the spirit is pure and under the special control and influence of the Lord, but the body is of the earth and is subject to the power of the devil and is under the mighty influence of that fallen nature that is of the earth. If the spirit yields to the body, the devil then has power to overcome both the body and spirit of that man and he loses both. (Brigham Young, JD 2:255-256.)

SPIRITS OF MEN ARE FULL GROWN

The Spirits of our children are immortal before they come to us, and their spirits, after bodily death, are like they were before they came. They are as they would have appeared if they had lived in the flesh, to grow to maturity or to develop their physical bodies to the full stature of their spirits. If you see one of your children that has passed away it may appear to you in the form in which you would recognize it, the form of childhood; but if it' came to you as a messenger bearing some important truth, it would perhaps come... in the stature of full-grown manhood...

The spirit of Jesus Christ was full-grown before he was born into the world; and so our children were full-grown and possessed their full stature in the spirit before they entered mortality, the same stature that they will possess after they have passed away from mortality, and as they will also appear after the resurrection, when they shall have completed their mission. (Joseph F. Smith, IE 21:570-571 .)

SPIRITS OF THE JUST

When men are prepared, they are better off to go hence .... The spirits of the just are exalted to a greater and more glorious work; hence they are blessed in their departure to the world of spirits. Enveloped in flaming fire, they are not far from us, and know and understand our thoughts, feelings, and motions, and are often pained therewith. (Joseph Smith, HC 6:52.)

RELATIONSHIP OF THE SPIRIT OF MAN TO HIS BODY

"How does brother Snow's spirit look when it is disembodied?" Why, you just look at me now, and you can answer the question. How does the spirit of my wife look? Why, just look at her and see. And if we were both disembodied at the same instant, we should scarcely know that we were changed any more than we would if we both started out of the door at the same instant and found ourselves outside, looking at each other, and do not see very much difference between us than what there was when we were both inside the house. Whether inside or out of it, we are the same beings. Conversing together? Yes. Looking at each other? Yes. The same features exactly. Our tabernacles are formed for our spirits, yes, expressly for our spirits. But why were they not all made alike? Why were they not all made just six feet high? And why were they not all, in every respect, all the same length; limbs, likeness, the same; the same length of an arm? You may just as well ask the tailor, "Why do you make different sized coats and pants?" And say to the milliner also, "Why do you make different sizes of dresses and other garments?" And their answer is, because I have so many different persons to fit, and I make the garment to fit the person. And that is the answer concerning the tabernacles. They are made to fit the spirits. (Erastus Snow, JD .19:273-274.)

SPIRITS ARE FAMILIAR WITH OTHER SPIRITS

Spirits are just as familiar with spirits as bodies are with bodies, though spirits are composed of matter so refined as not to be tangible to this coarser organization. (Brigham Young, JD 3:371-372.)

SPIRIT WORLD

WHERE IS THE SPIRIT WORLD?

Where is the spirit world? It is incorporated within this celestial system. Can you see it with your natural eyes? No. Can you see spirits in this room? No. Suppose the Lord should touch your eyes that you might see, could you then see the spirits? Yes, as plainly as you now see bodies, as did the servant of Elijah. If the Lord would permit it, and it was his will that it should be done, you could see the spirits that have departed from this world as plainly as you now see bodies with your natural eyes. (Brigham Young, JD 3:368.)

THE SPIRIT WORLD AS SEEN BY WILFORD WOODRUFF

I feel at liberty to reveal to this assembly this morning what has been revealed to me since we were here yesterday morning. If the veil could be taken from our eyes and we could see into the spirit world, we would see that Joseph Smith, Brigham Young and John Taylor had gathered together every spirit that ever dwelt in the flesh in this Church since its organization. We would also see the faithful apostles and elders of the Nephites who dwelt in the flesh in the days of Jesus Christ. In that assembly we would also see Isaiah and every prophet and apostle that ever prophesied of the great work of God. In the midst of these spirits we would see the Son of God, the Savior, who presides and guides and controls the preparing of the kingdom of God on the earth and in heaven. From that body of spirits, when we shout "Hosanna to God and the Lamb!" there is a mighty shout goes up of "Glory to God in the Highest!" that the God of Israel has permitted his people to finish this temple and prepare it for the great work that lies before the Latter-day Saints. These patriarchs and prophets who have wished for this day, rejoice in the spirit world that the day has come when the saints of the Most High God have had power to carry out this great mission. (Wilford Woodruff, A Book of Remembrance, 81-82.)

A VIEW OF THE SPIRIT WORLD

I went to see him [Jedediah M. Grant] one day last week, and he reached out his hand and shook hands with me; he could not speak, but he shook hands warmly with me ..... I laid my hands upon him and blessed him, and asked God to strengthen his lungs that he might be easier, and in two or three minutes he raised himself up and talked for about an hour as busily as he could, telling me what he had seen and what he understood, until I was afraid he would weary himself, when I arose and left him.

He said to me, "Brother Heber, I have been into the spirit world two nights in succession, and, of all the dreads that ever came across me, the worst was to have to again return to my body, though I had to do it. But O," says he, "the order and government that were there! When in the spirit world, I saw the order of righteous men and women; beheld them organized in their several grades, and there appeared to be no obstruction to my vision; I could see every man and woman in their grade and order. I looked